A JOURNEY TO NOWHERE

Also by Jean-Paul Kauffmann in English translation

The Dark Room at Longwood: A Voyage to St Helena (1999)

Voyage to Desolation Island (2001)

Wrestling with the Angel: The Mystery of Delacroix's Mural (2003)

JEAN-PAUL KAUFFMANN

A JOURNEY TO NOWHERE
Detours and Riddles
in the Lands and History of Courland

Translated from the French by
Euan Cameron

MACLEHOSE PRESS
QUERCUS · LONDON

First published in French as *Courlande* by Éditions Fayard, Paris, 2009
First published in Great Britain in 2012 by

MacLehose Press
an imprint of Quercus
55 Baker Street
7th Floor, South Block
London W1U 8EW

A CIP catalogue record for this book is available
from the British Library

ISBN 978 0 85705 036 6

10 9 8 7 6 5 4 3 2 1

Designed and typeset in Miller by Libanus Press, Marlborough
Printed and bound in Great Britain by Clays Ltd, St Ives plc

In memory of Ronald Moreau

CONTENTS

IV – THE HOUSE ON THE LAKE

V – THE RETURN

Markers in the text – *, †, ‡ – refer to notes on pp.261–5

*Courland appears to be a gentle land dedicated
from the beginning of the world to Virgilian peace and
where nothing ever happened.*

RENÉ PUAUX, *Portrait de la Lettonie* (1937)

THE BALTICS TODAY

THE FORMER COURLAND TODAY

PROLOGUE

Twenty or so caskets in a row. Coats of arms, metal rings, the upper parts in the shape of a trapezium. And the silence befitting a crypt: sarcophagi come instantly to mind. Yet there is nothing gloomy about the necropolis at the palace of Mitau. It is an illusion. The lids, badly fitted onto the caskets, leave gaps.

I try to make out what is hidden inside. One casket, the only one covered by a sheet, intrigues me. My guide has his back to me; he wants to turn the lights on and is fiddling with the electric meter in the corner. I take the opportunity to lift the dark-blue material. A coffin adorned with black velvet braid is revealed. The guide looms. He has spotted me; my number is up. It is as if I have desecrated a tomb. I have just profaned the monument to Duke Jacob of Courland (1610–1681).

But no, the guide is smiling, removing more of the crepe to better display the velvet-braided coffin. Inside it lie the remains of an unusual character, the man who made Courland an independent nation. This entrepreneurial prince signed a treaty with Louis XIV to mark the establishment of the Compagnie Française du Commerce du Nord. From Saint-Malo to Rochefort, ships from Courland, identifiable by their flag featuring a red crayfish on a black ground, sailed the length of the French coast. So active was his navy that the Duke of Courland tried to obtain a concession from the King of France to set up a base at Marennes. Receptive to new ideas and to international trade, the duke despatched ships to the Caribbean and to Africa. And so it was that by the end of the seventeenth century, Courland possessed two colonies: one in the West Indies, in Tobago; the other in Africa, on the island of Saint Andrew, in the estuary of the River Gambia.

The guide has managed to switch on the lights in the crypt. The sarcophagi are harshly illuminated, the fluorescent lights lending the vault a Hollywood aspect. The guide is coaxed into confirming what we already suspected: the sarcophagi are empty. A museum next door displays the desecration the Bolsheviks inflicted on these remains in 1919. Dragged from their lead-lined coffins, exposed to the ridicule of the crowd, the corpses of the dukes and their families were scattered. In *The Outlaws*, Ernst von Salomon describes the scene: "The embalmed corpses were discovered mockingly arrayed in German steel helmets, stood up against a wall and pumped full of lead by the maniacs' bullets." Hauled into the street, the mummified body of one Duke of Courland was tossed into the river, then dragged out again to be propped against a wall. They tried to hold him upright for use as a target by the crowd, which cheered when his skull exploded.

The formal attire worn by the mummified corpses when they were found is exhibited in the little museum. The decorative ribbons, hats and dresses displayed in the vitrines are in excellent condition, not in the least shabby. During the Terror, the corpses of the kings of France were wrenched from their tombs at Saint-Denis. The corpse of Henri IV, perfectly preserved, was propped against a pillar. The crowd plucked hairs from his white beard and kept them as souvenirs.

A few yards from the necropolis, the café welcomes students from the agricultural college. They look lost in the vast corridors of the castle, which was built by Rastrelli, the architect of the Winter Palace in St Petersburg. There is nothing to remind one of Louis XVIII, who spent some of his exile here, apart from a print depicting the monarch

14

and his niece, Madame Royale, wandering about in the snow, driven out of Mitau by Tsar Paul I.

Mitau is a palace of illusions. The building was destroyed in 1944. Everything, apart from its basic components, the foundations and the walls. And what walls! One of the most splendid examples of eighteenth-century European architecture, and God knows the era abounded in fine houses, mansions and palaces, most of them masterpieces.

Mitau is a mere façade. The mirage recalls the abstract grandeur of St Petersburg, the unreal solidity of certain buildings in Baltic Europe. Courland, where the most modest village boasts a manor house at the very least, is a good example of this: there, mansions have been destroyed, lie in ruins or are on the verge of collapse. Constructed by Germano-Baltic barons, they witnessed eventful times. I've never stopped encountering their secret past.

Courland belongs to my life, to my history. I set off in search of a name. I embarked upon the pursuit of a memory.

I

THIRTY YEARS LATER

MARA FROM CANADA

Her name was Mara,* usually written with a macron over the first "a". It all happened thirty years ago. I knew her in Montreal when I was completing my national service, doing voluntary work overseas. I was twenty-two. In order to pay the fees for her Modern Literature course at McGill University, Mara was working in a bookshop that I frequented from time to time. I noticed her immediately. How could one not? She was blonde and unusually beautiful – a term I do not use lightly – one of those radiant, shy Nordic beauties. Her attraction had a good deal to do with a lack of confidence. She did not know that she was beautiful. Despite her twenty years, her perfect features lent her a dignified air belied by a lack of guile that one could see straight away was not affected. In her ingenuousness, she was vaguely aware of the turmoil she inspired, but she appeared to have made up her mind not to take any notice.

I reckoned that I would have a hard time seducing her. In those days I was quite a daredevil. Quebec – "*La Belle Province*" as it was known – was emerging from two centuries of obscurantism. It was not difficult to break down the resistance of *Québécoise* girls, who had been completely freed of their inhibitions during the "peaceful revolution". I was not the only one to show an interest in Mara; there was a clear influx of customers on the days when she was working. I didn't realize this at first, but the way in which her admirers leafed mechanically through books while ogling her suggested a certain voyeurism, not in the least unwholesome incidentally, in that the individual concerned suspected nothing. This lack of awareness could eventually have become irksome. Was she so innocent, in fact? Yet you only had to ask her for information, the title of a book or the name of an author you couldn't remember, to realize that she was not dissembling. The sincerity in her voice rang true.

I had initially assumed Mara was a *Québécoise* because – even though she didn't have the characteristic accent of *"La Belle Province"* – certain turns of phrase, if you listened carefully, led you to suspect that French was not her mother tongue. I had deduced that she was an English-speaking Canadian, but this didn't quite tally.

In the bookshop, I enjoyed asking her questions to which I knew the answers, just to hear her voice, study her face close up and see how she coped. She was rarely caught out on the subject of post-war French literature. She had a good knowledge of Sartre, Simone de Beauvoir and Camus. De Beauvoir especially; Mara clearly admired her. How, I asked myself, could someone admire the author of *The Second Sex*, not exactly a wide-eyed innocent, quite so much and be as naïve as Mara was? What is more, she discussed de Beauvoir's work intelligently, within the strict limits of her studies, without ever expressing an opinion that might give her away. Her attitude wasn't premeditated; she was naturally shy. She was less reliable on the nineteenth century, though well informed about Hugo, Stendhal, Balzac, Flaubert, de Maupassant and Zola. Stendhal was her favourite. She knew his entire oeuvre, even the little-known *Les Privilèges*, a short essay she suggested I read. I found it hard to understand how such a respectable girl could have recommended a book in which Stendhal imagines having all his unmentionable, perverted desires satisfied. (I recently came across this work, which consists of twenty-three paragraphs. Article 3 concerns the *mentula*, "like the pointed finger for hardness and movement, on demand". At the time, I was not aware that this *mentula* is none other than the phallus, and that Stendhal was writing about masturbation. Was Mara unaware of this too?)

I tried to embarrass her by asking complicated or inappropriate questions. She responded with the patience of an angel and a desire to say the right thing that compelled admiration. I did my best to embellish my questions with jokes and innuendo, but she always ignored them. The boundary between her work and her private life would not be breached. This quiet determination intrigued me. Did she have a lover? Apparently not. No young man was ever waiting for her outside the bookshop. At 7.15 p.m., she would catch the bus a few blocks away and make her way home.

One day when I was giving up hope of being able to break down Mara's reticence, I chanced upon her in one of the city's parks. She was sitting on a bench, leafing through a book. Without asking permission, I sat down beside her. The book she was reading was by de Beauvoir. I can still remember the title – *Pour une morale de l'ambiguïté* – which did not accord, to say the least, with Mara's own clear-cut personality. I asked her what she liked about de Beauvoir. Was Mara a feminist? Her replies were trite and noncommittal: "I like her style"; "She describes her characters so well", etc. Nothing could shake Mara's self-control. My cause was hopeless. I had to face the facts: I was not her type.

I was about to get up when she asked what the book was that I had in my hand. Feeling slightly ashamed, I showed it to her. It was a biography of Louis XVIII, hardly the most fashionable of monarchs. Louis XIV, Napoleon I, might just about pass muster, but this plump, totally unpretentious Bourbon? I was a compulsive reader; I would read everything that fell into my hands. It is also true that at that

21

time the period following the fall of Napoleon interested me more than the Empire. The Restoration of the Bourbon Monarchy is the literary period par excellence. The confrontation of the old monarchic order and the new world occurred precisely during the reigns of Louis XVIII and Charles X. It is this shift that forms the backdrop to the novels of Balzac and Stendhal.

I grudgingly showed Mara the book. The gout-plagued king would certainly not improve my lot with her. Did she even know who he was?

"Louis XVIII? How extraordinary! He lived in my country."

She must have been mistaken. Be that as it may, I had never seen her look that way before. Her face lit up at last! This vivaciousness accentuated her features, lending them an almost sensual harmony.

"What do you mean, in your country? Louis XVIII lived in Paris, at the Tuileries. The palace was burned down during the Commune."

"Yes, but before the Tuileries."

Her expression was transformed. It was not that she had been inscrutable or even sullen before; she presented a pleasant, if impersonal, demeanour to everyone. No . . . what struck me at that moment was that she was no longer on the defensive. She pronounced "Les Tuileries" oddly, as "les Tueries", or something similar.

"Before that, well, I think he wandered around Europe. He lived in exile during the Revolution and the Empire. He lived where anyone would have him."

"Look it up in your book. He took refuge in my country, in Courland."

To tell the truth, I had only just started the book: the childhood at Versailles; the rivalry with his brother, the future Louis XVI; his marriage to the daughter of the King of Sardinia. I can't pretend that the figure of this somewhat hypocritical prince enthralled me.

Courland ... the name must have made an impression, though I can't be certain. Its appeal had much to do with Mara. Without her, would the word have attracted me in the same way? Courland ... Phonetically, its French pronunciation gave off a particular shading, more precisely a shimmering effect that I associated with embroidery, with flounced ribbons hung in festoons. These connections were not unfounded, as I was to realize later: during the summer solstice celebrations, girls in Courland wear floral crowns while boys dress up in oak leaves. Courland adorns itself with pagan decorations, making the country resemble one of those barbaric Northern kingdoms.

"Aren't you Canadian?"

A stupid question. In North America, people always come from somewhere else, even if, after several generations, parts of the population have lost all traces of their origins. The *Québécois* are an exception; virtually all of the descendants of the 60,000 French men and women who remained in Canada after the defeat of 1759 know where their forebears had set sail from.

"I am Canadian," she said, cut to the quick.

Her parents had become assimilated into the English-speaking population. At the time I did not know where Courland was, but there was no question of my confessing my ignorance. I was more or less certain that it was somewhere in Northern Europe, but was incapable of saying whether or not it was an independent nation. I risked nothing by asking about the circumstances in which she had left.

"I don't know my homeland, alas. I was born in Germany. At the end of the war, my parents left their country clandestinely aboard a fishing boat, taking refuge on the island of Gotland, in Sweden, before moving on to West Germany. They stayed for seven years, convinced that the Soviet occupation was not going to last. Like many Latvians,

23

my parents were convinced that right was on their side. They probably thought that international pressure would force the Russians to retire behind the frontiers fixed at the time of independence. One of my uncles stayed put. He was a member of the Brothers of the Forest, an anti-Soviet resistance movement. He disappeared without a trace. It was at that time that my parents decided to leave Europe and settle in Canada. They had realized that Latvia was not going to regain its sovereignty."

The Brothers of the Forest: I imagined a band of Robin Hoods repeatedly attacking the occupying forces. The truth, I would learn later, was nowhere near as entertaining as Walter Scott.

All these details provided by a now loquacious Mara meant that the polite indifference she had shown me was starting to disperse. I wasn't just anybody. It was that old fatty, Louis XVIII, whom I had to thank for this. He suddenly struck me as rather attractive. But the game was far from won. Mara's indifference might have disappeared, but it had given way to a wariness bordering on mistrust. I felt that she was waiting for something to happen. Today I reckon that she was right to be on her guard. Courland was her weak spot; one did not need to be a great strategist to realize that this was the direction in which to attack.

It was not easy in those days to obtain information about such a subject. Google did not exist. The details provided in dictionaries and encyclopaedias were scant. There was no book about Courland in the library, apart from one or two biographies of Dorothea of Courland, Duchess of Dino, a character I had foolishly overlooked. A duchess *after* Louis XVIII! I told myself that I was not going to win Mara over with one of these characters from the past. One of the many strange things about Courland – yet another discovery I was to make later –

was Dorothea's unusualness. Although not beautiful, she possessed, according to her contemporaries, an uncanny charm. Nicknamed the "Circe of Europe", she was, moreover, endowed with exceptional intelligence. Dorothea gave Talleyrand a helping hand at the Congress of Vienna. His principal assistant, she was probably also his mistress.

THE *"GRAND ORAL"*

My voluntary stint overseas having come to an end, I extended my stay in Quebec, for Mara's sake, by working for a magazine. Every self-respecting newspaper at the time was equipped with a sizeable information department, so I asked the one where I was employed for help. It wasn't for lack of searching: I could find nothing about Courland. Until the day that a *recherchiste* – which is what they are called in Quebec – advised me to look under "Latvia". This revelation, however useful, provided me with no information of any substance except for two or three facts. I discovered that Courland corresponded to Latvia's coastal area, and that the Soviets kept a particularly close watch on that coastline. I was naturally keen to flaunt my recently acquired knowledge to my lovely *Courlandaise*. She was not in the least impressed. She may have been innocent, but she was no fool. She knew very well that my curiosity was not disinterested. But I think she was touched by my persistence and my eagerness to find out more.

She displayed the same impartiality at the bookshop. The only difference was that I was permitted to wait for her when she left work and to accompany her as far as the bus stop, to the great indignation of my rivals, who prowled around the shop aware that I was gaining the advantage with every passing day. When the bus arrived, I would jump aboard. This astonished her.

She didn't let it show, but the tone in which she said, "You're totally crazy" made me feel that I was making progress.

However many points I accumulated, though, I was not gaining much ground. This bantering could have gone on for weeks, even months. I was patient. I had postponed my return to France for Mara's sake. Merely being able to talk to her, to have a casual relationship with her – all relative, it is true – to be able to gaze at her at my ease rather than ogle her surreptitiously as all those other voyeurs did, was enough to make me happy.

It is possible that my confidence may have secretly irritated Mara. I was convinced that a new stage would be reached, that it was merely a question of waiting. She was quite capable of sending me packing, yet she did not do so. She allowed me a few liberties, such as kissing her goodbye – at that time one didn't kiss just anyone on the cheek. These ruses, which seem very old-fashioned today, fostered an atmosphere that already had something of a flirtation or lovers' intimacy about it. From the way people looked at her, Mara was beginning to have an inkling of the seductive power she had been unaware of until then. I was launched on the divine pursuit described by writers I respected. And she felt that she was being admired. While remaining aloof, she was probably grateful to me for this discovery. We talked a great deal. Everything was conspiring to nurture that mutual knowledge through which we each received a magnified image of the other.

She still refused to come up to my room. We spent hours at a time, in the evening, sitting on the staircase in the dark. I held her hand. She loved me massaging her palm and responded with long, gentle squeezes. One day, she brought me a book. Even though she worked in a bookshop and was well versed in French literature, this book was an unexpected choice for an English-speaking Canadian, even though, in the late 1960s, the author was far from unknown.

"I take no credit," Mara said. "The book is set in Courland in 1919–20,

27

when the Bolsheviks were occupying our country and the Germans were trying to create an independent territory called Baltikum."

The book was Marguerite Yourcenar's *Coup de grâce*,* which had been published a few months before the start of the Second World War. It is the story of three young Germano-Baltic aristocrats cut off with German commandos in a mansion in Courland surrounded by Bolsheviks. I enjoyed the twilight world the story depicted. There was something desperate about these besieged characters in the midst of a wintry landscape. If Mara did not care for the book, it was out of exaggerated pride: "Those Baltic barons did a good deal of harm to Courland." I objected that the background was of secondary importance. All that mattered was the love affair between Sophie and Eric.

Mara evaded this remark. She had no wish to discuss those characters' equivocal feelings, which would, I imagine, have forced her towards certain discoveries about herself.

The fact that a country should have crystallized feelings of love may scarcely seem credible nowadays. Embellished with every splendour, Courland was becoming a fabled land for both of us, all the more unreal because Mara had never set foot there. She was literally overwhelmed by her origins. Yet she was no longer a child. She could easily have escaped the hold her family had on her, which must have been burdensome. At the time, this didn't cross my mind. We were being crushed by the weight of tradition. "The old world is exhausted, let's ready our ships": I had pinned Max Jacob's remark above my work table, proof that we had not yet succeeded in setting sail.

Mara felt Canadian, that went without saying. She had no sense of being an exile. I assumed that in this respect she was different from her parents, who had waited in vain for the situation to improve before setting out for the New World. Had they relinquished their homeland for good? She often spoke about them. They had apparently settled in without difficulty. The father was a wealthy businessman who worked in the aeronautics field. The mother was a housewife. Mara had two younger sisters. The family lived in the smart district of Outremont.

One day Mara announced that her parents had invited me to a Mid-summer's Day party. This celebration of the summer solstice is Latvia's most important annual festival. The invitation struck me as being just like our important oral exam in France, known as the *"grand oral".**

"The *grand oral*! But it will be very easy! You French people express yourselves so well."

I haven't mentioned that being addressed as *tu* also featured among the points accumulating in my favour. Mara did not know about the French *grand oral*.

"The *grand oral* is an exam. Do you think that your parents will pass or fail me?"

"They're not like that. I'm sure you'll like them."

I was a bit anxious. Things were getting serious. What plot were Mara and her family hatching? It was all the more intriguing since nothing had happened between us. Was it a trap? But I was ready to do anything to please Mara.

The great day arrived. I rang the doorbell. The wait seemed endless. I was about to ring again when the door opened. A woman, an older version of Mara, appeared, her head wreathed in flowers. Her beauty was just as disturbing as her daughter's. Like Mara, she lacked ease and assurance. There was a certain stiffness to her manner that lent coldness to her face and, at the same time, true perfection. The flowers on her head, however, belied her stern expression. The wreaths worn by Mara and her sisters were less lavish, seeming to indicate that it was

29

the mother who wore the crown whereas the three daughters had been allotted mere tiaras.

It was a rare sight, and is for ever imprinted on my memory. Long afterwards, when admiring paintings by Botticelli, I often thought of the four women in Montreal. The comparison was not entirely apt. The artist's goddesses and madonnas belong to the Florentine world. The purity of their faces and their finery is restrained, which was not the case with the four Courland graces, Nordic beauties whose features were at once compact and seemingly weightless, with something indestructible about them. The two younger girls still had a delicate freshness, though they resembled Mara and their mother in their robust, vaguely chilly expressions, and there was an almost barbaric magnificence about them. I did not know at the time that this feast of Saint John had its origins in a pagan festival, the *ligo*. It was not a Christian saint whom the Latvians were celebrating but the sun god.

What a splendid evening it was! When the mother began to sing a sort of lament, the rest of the family took up the chorus. I discovered later that this recitation was a *daina*, a short poem that describes the secret of the human adventure. A sort of bible for the Latvians, the *daina* has played a vital role in maintaining national pride.

It was harder to determine what sort of man the father was. I realized much later that his courteousness, his apparently good-natured manner and his jokes were means by which he took advantage of the person to whom he was talking. In fact, he never stopped observing people, testing them, sizing them up. Behind his shyness, one sensed a troubled spirit. Smiling and ruthless, he reminded me of a character in a Bergman film – it was the period of *Persona*: "You desire my daughter, this treasure whom Heaven and I myself have created? I know that she must leave us one day. I have been preparing for it for a long time.

I have enough influence over her to get rid of suitors whom I do not like. You, clearly, are not ready." Such must have been the thoughts of Mara's father. At least, that is what I imagine them to have been. I remember, too, how brazen I was in those days, how totally trusting. I had also drunk a great deal of the Latvian speciality known as "black balsam", a deceptively strong liqueur made from berries, herbs and spices.

"My parents liked you very much," Mara told me the following morning.

Later, she would confess that this was untrue. Her parents had made no comment. Paradoxically, this lack of any reaction, tantamount to a negative response, worked in my favour. Was this Mara's first act of rebellion against her family? It is possible; her attitude had certainly changed. She was considerably more relaxed. Later, she would say, "As far as I'm concerned, you passed the *grand oral*."

A week after her parents' invitation, Mara became my lover. In truth, I had not expected it, at least not so soon. She had taken the initiative by suggesting that we go to my place, having previously refused my invitations. What had happened? Even today, I wonder about this surrender. I could not help questioning her on the matter. She claimed that before the party at her parents' home, she had not been sure about me, but, watching me with her family, she had realized that she was in love with me. The problem was that I have only a hazy memory of that evening. I wonder what it was that had won her over.

"Beware of Frenchmen; they are libertines." Mara's notion of France had been formed largely through her reading. She thought that we were all schemers like Julien Sorel, or perverts like Lucien de Rubempré. "You're all debauched", she would often say. I find it difficult to imagine what would have led her to think of me as being immoral. I was not in the least. She, on the other hand, astonished me. To begin with, she was not a virgin.

31

In those early days of sexual liberation, there was nothing surprising about that. Being aware of her earlier attitude and her good-natured lack of response, however, I was momentarily nonplussed. I did not dwell on the fact – I even found it curiously comforting – that such a solemn and delicate act could have been accomplished by someone else.

I was amazed by the transformation in Mara; I no longer recognized my *Courlandaise*. How could the shy, inhibited person of those early days have turned into this resourceful, totally unconstrained creature? Sex with her was an intense moment of surrender and exultant passion, totally free of any sense of original sin. She had a brazen beauty. I nicknamed her after the Spanish *maja* so dear to Goya; it pleased her immensely to be compared to his *Maja desnuda* in the Prado. Not that she looked like Goya's *maja*, who is dark-haired, has a small waist and is slightly plump; Mara was tall, blond and slender. Although she was proud of her real name (Mara is the chief goddess of the ancient Latvians), it amused her to hear it pronounced in the guttural Spanish way.

Mara regarded lovemaking as a natural exercise, something pleasurable, which it undoubtedly is, but not solely. Being more romantic, I was probably dreaming of an impossible merging of soul and body. I did not criticize her, but had she really benefited from reading Stendhal and Balzac's portrayals of introspective love? If so, what had she retained?

The months I spent with Mara were among the most carefree of my life. I loved to hear her sing. She hummed the songs of her homeland in a soothing and melancholy voice. I adored this strange language and its inflexions, which were both hard and muffled. "There is nothing sad in these songs. They are about man's happiness in harmony with nature", she would say. Sometimes I asked her to translate them. They were to do with the sun, the wind, the water, presented as characters in every-day life.

I again delayed my departure for France. For a while, I even considered staying on in Canada, but one thing put me off: the endless winter with its continuous snow. This whiteness, which blanks out all shapes and brings everything to a standstill, is for me the colour of desolation.

I hesitated. Strangely enough, it was Mara who made me decide to leave Montreal. As I have indicated, she, unlike her parents, did not feel in the least bothered about being cut off from her native land. But the atmosphere at home had engendered a sense of loss, a lack of fulfilment, which, I felt sure, affected her sensibility.

Yet everything was so simple where she was concerned! Too simple, perhaps. I remember only too well the day I told her that I was going back to France. It was April. There were still patches of snow in the streets, and, as always at that time of year, snowstorms were interspersed with milder spells of weather, making the pavements slushy. That day she was wearing an elegant fur hat that made her irresistible. I walked beside her, mesmerized by this beautiful Nordic Diana, by her flowing stride, by her riding boots that accentuated the nonchalant air she had acquired since she had become my lover. She burst into tears, asserting that, like all Frenchmen, I was degenerate: "Now you've got what you want, you're dropping me!"

I comforted her by telling her that she could come to France. I was not abandoning her. Had she not expressed the intention to spend a year studying in Paris? I was leaving to prepare for her arrival.

It was not an abrupt separation. We would write to one another and see each other soon. I was sincere. She pretended to believe me.

CIRCE

Never ... Love stories need conclusive words so that we should not forget them.

I never saw her again.

Our letters became less and less frequent until, after eight or nine months, they stopped completely. I'd begun a new life. It was impossible to know what had happened to Mara.

I think of her often. She is the symbol of my Canadian period, my younger days, the image of a certain perfection and lost innocence. My memories of her survive on account of Courland. For thirty years, my brain has automatically registered any information having to do with that country, a more or less conscious appropriation of data that has gradually extended to all of Latvia. There's no doubt that I left part of myself in Canada. This represented neither desertion nor absence. I became unaccustomed to Mara; I did not forget her. The memories have not died, but her colours have faded. Therefore the word *Courland*, which I associate with my beautiful bookseller, continues to transmit hazy signals in my memory. A vague lookout system operates in my brain. It is related to the frivolity of my youth and the distinctive qualities of that unaffected girl who taught me to make the most of every moment.

After being away for over three years, I readjusted to living in France without too much difficulty, though not without a certain sense of remorse, which I quickly dismissed when I remembered that Mara was just as forgetful as I was. I would be reminded of her a few years later, without her being aware of the fact, by a television serial, *La Demoiselle d'Avignon*. At that time, there were only three channels in France. Twenty million viewers were enthralled by the love affair between Koba and François Fonsalette, played by Marthe Keller and Louis Velle. Koba, the foreign student, was in reality a princess from the North: Kristina de Kurlande. This semi-fictional land was reminiscent of a Scandinavian kingdom, but the coincidence was disconcerting, particularly since Marthe Keller much resembled Mara. Without exactly looking like her, she possessed the same radiant freshness, the same delicate, sculptural beauty, and her accent reminded me of Mara's. The princess from Kurlande wore a ring that was almost identical to the one I had given Mara before my departure; it symbolized the union between her country and the sea. I could not help thinking of Duke Jacob, who had dragged Courland into its maritime adventures long ago. Then the television serial came to an end.

I accumulated a great deal of information about Courland in a disorderly way. I still had fond feelings for Louis XVIII. In the 1980s, I was fascinated by the work of Marguerite Yourcenar;* I even called on her on her island of Mount Desert. The meeting was not a success. During those years, I also discovered the remarkable figure of the Duchess of Dino, as well as her no less extraordinary sister, the Princess of Sagan.

When I was working at *Le Matin de Paris*, there was a young woman who intrigued me. She never spoke to anyone, and she would cross the newsroom in a great hurry to get to her office, which was on the top floor. Her expression was impenetrable, but she stood out because of an elegance and natural ease that discouraged all forms of familiarity. There was nothing surprising about her stylish manner, since she was responsible for the newspaper's fashion column. Her first name was Dorothée. I eventually made her acquaintance. I had been mistaken: she was affability personified. Sweet yet determined, and not easily influenced, she went steadily about her job with a lack of affectation that lent her a good deal of charm: "When I don't know someone, I assume a mask of indifference. This is the essence of civility." Although this is how she behaved, in actual fact she was very sociable. When you got to know her, her mask fell away and her apparent lack of receptivity disappeared completely. She observed the menagerie at *Le Matin* with amusement. Many of the staff tried to chat her up, not in the least deterred by her "snooty" manner. Which must have run in the family. Reading a biography of the Duchess of Dino, I discovered that Dorothée was a direct descendant of Dorothea of Courland.

"I didn't know that you were interested in her," she said.

I replied that it was Courland that interested me.

"Believe it or not, I've never been there. My father insisted on giving me the name Dorothée. What do you think of her?"

Yet another *Courlandaise* who had never set foot in her own country! I told her what I knew about her forebear, the great seductress nicknamed the "Circe of Europe". Had she not succeeded in casting a spell on Talleyrand? I suspect that Dorothée knew just as much as I did, if not more, about her ancestor. She was testing me.

In 1991, the independence of the Baltic states, of which Latvia was one, resonated with me, but that was all. "Mara must be pleased", I must have said to myself.

This section of my Courland memoir must resemble an antique shop, an array of objects, circumstances and impressions that I have never thought of labelling or putting in order. It has become a topic about which my wife Joëlle teases me and which comes up now and then. I have told her about Mara. What was the reality of this love affair?

When I informed Joëlle that I had accepted a commission to write a feature article about Courland, she said, "I'd love to see the place. I hope you'll take me with you."

That had not been part of the plan. But why not?

WHERE IS COURLAND?

Henri S. is one of my oldest friends. We went to journalism school together in Lille. He enjoys an excellent reputation within the profession; I have watched him rise steadily to the top. Henri has always progressed upwards: department manager, deputy editor-in-chief, editor-in-chief ... Managing staff is his métier. At present, he is editorial director of a travel magazine. He is a born leader, never has to make demands or put constraints on people. The journalists who work for him, a highly sensitive lot, are grateful. There is no-one quite like him when it comes to reassuring them, massaging their egos or cheering them up.

Henri is an old fox without any illusions, a slightly world-weary man who has lived on his reputation for forty years. He is seen as being indispensable, the good mechanic who can fix anything and get one out of trouble. All of the proprietors of the large newspaper groups think of him when one of their publications is going through a difficult period. Henri resolves nothing, but he restores confidence in editors, readers and shareholders alike. Conflicts suddenly abate; in the majority of cases, sales pick up again. The method is tried and tested. Henri is no fool. This is what makes him likeable. My old friend is probably an impostor but of the most lovable kind; he is neither spineless nor arrogant. We frequently have lunch together. Sometimes he tries out ideas on me, but imagination is not his forte. His strength is to make himself useful with remarkable discretion. Lots of common sense but few ideas. It is usually his assistants who come up with the ideas. His free-lancers too. "I'm fortunate to have them; they're the salt of the earth. But as soon as I give them contracts, they dry up," he says with a sigh.

One day Henri said to me, "We are preparing a special issue on the Baltic states. My reporters have run out of ideas. I keep saying that they shouldn't deal with them country by country. That's not interesting. In any case, people confuse the countries. I sometimes get mixed up myself. Vilnius is the capital of Latvia, isn't it?"

"Of Lithuania, actually."

"You see the problem! This is why I've suggested a transverse approach."

"'Transverse'?"

"The Russian-speaking minorities, for example ... That's all I've come up with so far. Can you help me out here?"

"I know something about Courland, but that hardly fits with what you're looking for. It's not 'transversal'."

"Courland ..."

He grew thoughtful. I have often noticed that people become thoughtful when this name is mentioned. Probably because of the sonority, which is both unusual and familiar. It is the name of a foreign country and vaguely suggests something, but what?

"Put me in the picture, will you? As far as I know, Courland is part of one of the three Baltic countries. I bet it's in Estonia."

"Wrong again. It's in Latvia."

I tell him what I know about Courland, which is not much. I allude to the manor houses of the Baltic barons. He interrupts me: "Real manor houses, like in Brittany? That's great. At least it will mean something to people. Can one visit them?"

I say that I don't know. He is disappointed.

"I thought you knew the country."

"I know it, but I've never set foot there."

"Explain yourself! I don't follow."

"You can be obsessed by a country without having been there. In my childhood, for example, it was the Kerguelen Islands. I collected masses of information about that archipelago. I knew everything, or almost everything, up until the day I went there."*

"Once you were there, obviously, it wasn't anything like what you had learned."

"Not at all. It was identical to what I had imagined in every way."

"So you made a useless journey?"

"Essentially there were no surprises. The thrill was in the details, the circumstances. That's probably why one travels: for the incidentals, the random events."

Henri is totally impervious to this type of nonsense, otherwise he would not be where he is.

"This is what I suggest: go to Courland. For as long as you want. As far as an angle is concerned, I trust your judgement. I realize the trip is pointless since you already know the country, but at least you will bring back some details, some superfluous stuff. That's what I want, understand? Inessentials!"

Henri is not always the person I think he is. He has a sense of the paradoxical. Sometimes he amazes me. He is more complex than he appears. He can occasionally have outbursts of nonconformism. It is probably due to this unpredictability that he endures. His proposal caught me unawares. Did I really want to make such a journey?

In the old days, I would not have hesitated.

THE RESURRECTOR APPEARS

I am happy to call her "my cousin"; I know she loves it when I do so. Sometimes she uses this relationship to put pressure on me. We have known one another for about ten years. She first got in touch after one of my genuine first cousins did some genealogical research.

My great-grandfather Michel Kauffmann emigrated to the region of Vitré, on the borders of Brittany, following the annexation of Alsace-Lorraine by Germany. His brothers remained at home. In 1918, when Alsace became French again, he did not get back in touch with his family. I don't know why. The only link was with his brothers, but all of them had died long since. My cousin is the great-granddaughter of one of them. That gives an idea of how distant the link is between us. However, the fact that we have a great-grandfather in common is enough to encourage complicity, even understanding, the artificial nature of which is obvious. Elisabeth gets in touch whenever she comes to Paris. My cousin passes for a woman of character, and rightly so. She is one of those domineering people whom men are happy to rely on: she takes care of everything, including the chores. There is no-one quite like her when it comes to deciding which play to see or reserving a good table at a restaurant. Evidently, her husband and children, who prefer to remain in Alsace, are not unhappy about her forays to Paris.

We see one another fairly frequently, yet we are not sufficiently close that I keep Elisabeth informed of my every move. But, having had to bow out of a concert – it was she, of course, who had succeeded in obtaining tickets – I thought it wise to explain why: I was getting ready to go off to Courland. I reckoned that, like nine out of ten people, she would ask me where Courland was. This is a game I play, not without a certain degree of sadism; it can probably also be seen as the ultimate in pedantry. Well, Elisabeth knew all about Courland. She did not care a damn about Louis XVIII's exile or the Baltic barons, but she was far better informed about recent history than I was.

"The Courland Pocket: does that mean anything to you?"

"Vaguely. The Germans occupied the region until May 1945, but I don't know any more. My word, you seem to know this pocket rather well!"

"I'm Alsatian. Alsace, the Second World War, the Wehrmacht . . . the '*malgré-nous*' . . ."*

I interrupt her. She has adopted that indignant tone which does not bode well. I already know what she is about to say: the *malgré-nous* who were forcibly enrolled in the German army, who were victimized, a disgrace for France. Why are they denied their proper status?

"What have the *malgré-nous* got to do with you?"

"My father was killed in Courland in 1945. His body was never found. We've never stopped searching. It's complicated. You must help me . . ."

"Help you how? If it's so important, why haven't you gone there yourself? Surely you weren't waiting for me to make investigations for you!"

"It was impossible to obtain information during the Soviet era. They destroyed many German graves. Since independence, it's become easier. I'm frightened of going. I no longer feel brave enough for that kind of adventure."

She spoke in a pleading little voice that I had not encountered before. Her normal imperious tone had vanished.

In advance of my departure, she put together some documents, insisting in particular that I track down the "Resurrector".

"What's all this? What Resurrector? Does he raise the dead?"

"That's what he's called; it's nothing to do with me. He's an Alsatian, he identifies abandoned graves; there are lots of them all over Courland. He's a true detective. Rediscovering long-deserted graves, verifying the identities of the dead – it's a way of resurrecting them, isn't it?"

"It's a curious title."

"I've never met him, but I know that he reports to the V.D.K."

"Never heard of it."

"The Volksbund Deutsche Kriegsgräberfürsorge, a German organization that looks after military cemeteries. Its headquarters are in Kassel."

Elisabeth suddenly regained her usual mocking tone.

"None of this explains why you are going to Courland."

43

II

THE JOURNEY TO COURLAND

A RED SKODA FAVORIT

In a few minutes' time the plane will land in Riga. A hellish programme has been arranged for me. Like Hermann Melville, suddenly I feel prey to that disease of modern travellers known as scepticism. Melville, who died in 1891, had nothing to complain about. In his day the planet still hid its hand; it could conjure up surprises.

Is Courland such a good idea? At this moment I feel annoyed with that wily old fox Henri, who succeeded in getting round me: "It's the world capital of Art Nouveau! You'll have to stay two or three days at least."

I have no wish to linger in Riga. I leave Joëlle in Alberta Street so that she can admire the façades designed by Mikhail Eisenstein, father of the film director. All that interests me is the outdoor ethnographic museum, situated on the outskirts of the city. The entire Latvian heritage has been assembled in this park, which stretches over almost 100 hectares. Farms, barns, cowsheds, stables, churches and windmills from every province in the land have been dismantled and rebuilt to be exhibited in this village created before the Second World War. Only the Courland section holds my attention. It is absurd, I realize, to disregard the culture of other regions. Straight away, I notice that I am avoiding Latvia. Had the Duchy of Courland not existed, would Latvia have become a state? Seen from Western Europe, the Baltic countries seem tiny, a sort of northern Benelux. In actual fact, Latvia, with its

64,000 square kilometres, is much larger than Belgium, Denmark or even Switzerland, but it has only 2.5 million inhabitants.

I discover a Lutheran church dating from the early eighteenth century. My first contact with Courland! I am reeling from the shock. But it's scarcely worth the effort: it's pathetically bare and gloomy, with everything locked away. The vaulted ceiling depicts Paradise. The celestial empire seems more like a place of mortification. The altar, the benches, the pulpit – everything suggests economies and austerity. A shaft of light from the ogive windows casts pale geometric figures on the floor. This black-and-white effect reminds me of a Carl Dreyer film: an interplay of grace and despair.

The encounter shocks me. Is this Courland? Brooding over this first reaction – which has taken me thirty years to bring about – I suddenly realize that this is a world that is possibly not meant for me. I tell myself that I am only in Riga, that this is merely a museum. The real encounter has yet to happen.

Suppose that this country that I have invented for myself does not correspond to reality! I walk inside a fisherman's house. How severe it is! Chest, wardrobe, bed, table, lobster pot, loom: no embellishments. Anything that is not functional has been excluded. This starkness does not appear to have been dictated by destitution or poverty. Every object, every detail, was created with relentless precision, efficiency and opportunism.

"Well?" Joëlle says on my return.

I do not really feel like sharing my disappointment.

"How about you?"

"You really missed something. I've never seen anything like it. Such abundance . . ."

"You were lucky. For me, it was the total opposite. Such frugality

. . . Between you and me, Courland is possibly not going to be very jolly."

Eventually I tell her about the park. She regrets not having come with me. I must be recounting things badly, or incorrectly. She says, "This bareness you describe, it's interesting." Protesting, I try to be more precise. Then, having run out of arguments, I hear myself saying, "It's the opposite of Italy." The comparison is foolish, particularly since we have not yet set foot in Courland. For us, Italy is the land of luxury par excellence. I am speaking, of course, about true luxury, the sort that can neither be bought nor acquired: a unique concentration of beauty. The profusion and the delicacy of colour. The wonderfully balanced tension between constraint and freedom. As far as I am aware, the Italians are the only people who still know how to relate the rules they apply to artistic creation to the way they dress, the way they furnish their homes and the way they eat.

"If Courland is the opposite of Italy, we won't be disappointed. Opposing values always come together. You've said so yourself. Your Courland may be the reverse image of Italy."

"Without wishing to make a play on the words *reverse* and *opposite*, they're not the same thing. I should like it to be a reverse image. 'My Courland', as you put it, is starting to worry me . . ."

We set off early from Riga in the direction of Liepaja (Libau in German). This former naval port, built in 1890 by Tsar Alexander III, was, until 1994, a Soviet military base that was out of bounds to the public, including Latvians.

I am driving a red Skoda Favorit, the 1988 model. The man from whom I hired it imagined that he was dispelling my fears by promising me that Skodas were superior to Ladas, which did not exactly reassure

49

me. The Lada is the worst car in the world; it is without doubt the model that has given rise to the greatest number of bad jokes ("Why do Ladas have a de-icer on the rear window? So that, in winter, your hands don't get cold when you push it").

An unadorned road lined with forests. From time to time a man appears along the verge, sitting stoically on a folding stool behind a stall displaying bottles of fruit juice. These stalls, which make one think of summer, seem by preference to be situated in the most deserted spots. Nobody stops.

"That's it, we're in Courland," Joëlle says, as she peruses the road map.

We pass a dilapidated boundary stone at the top of a small hill. Joëlle lowers her right arm solemnly, pointing her index finger as if she were starting a race. Kurzeme, Kurland. Courland, the land of the Cours.

"Honestly, I don't see any difference."

"What! Look, the forest is majestic. And the light. Don't you find that the light is different?"

"You're making fun of me."

She knows my weakness for emblems and signs: the symbolic crossing, the founding gesture, the first act, when in actual fact nothing has happened. I very much like this nothingness, this absence of material things. I dread the need to fill the void, to delight in the commonplace, to accentuate triteness.

I like these magical bits of evidence that denote a beginning, an opening like the raising of a curtain. I am foolish enough to believe that the course of an event is dependent on the quality of the opening, that the kick-off confers a definite value on what is to follow. I don't know

50

whether this entry into Courland on a badly tarmacked road bodes well. The route is still just as monotonous. Tracks jut into the forest at regular intervals. There is a sense of stillness, of absence, but this emptiness is not a loss. It merely needs to be filled. This vacant space is suspended, waiting. Closed-down factories, ruins, deserted farms: the end of a war. A particular kind of conflict, both dreary and cruel. The Soviets have left. I see this as a sort of internal cold war. The opponents were not equally matched.

The power lines are still entangled with the past. Poorly connected, they are held together by knots, by splicing. The twisted or amputated cables dangle, have been endlessly mended, and are badly coiled, divided and distended; some of them lie on the ground. The Skoda is well suited to this flat countryside, but at the slightest incline she loses power.

There is something about the scenery, in which fields and forests now alternate, that I am unable to pin down. Disharmony, anomaly – unless it is a beauty that is impossible to define. This distinctive quality nestles somewhere among the outlines of the landscape. But where?

In the distance is a grey shimmer: the Baltic. The first glimpse of the "Mediterranean of the North"; a murky, not very appealing sound of lapping water. There is a path down to the sea. A fishing boat is sunk into the sand. The beach is deserted. Dreary dunes. The unbroken shore is a white line without any distinguishing feature, lacking an *impression*. Long rhizomes creep over the foreshore. Bindweed, moss and lichens. Nets are drying on the beach. Water filters beneath the sand, leaving patterns. Above the shoreline, dunes studded with lyme-grass stretch as far as the eye can see.

A farm hides behind the dune, with its vegetable plot and chicken run. The garden is sunk deep into the soil, sheltered from the sea winds. It is 7.00 in the evening. A girl is picking broad beans, carrying a yellow plastic bucket in one hand. She is wearing a long, not very elegant blue dress, hippy-style, but her pale, delicate face does not fit the rustic surroundings. She is singing and contemplating each bean pod as she picks it, holding it between thumb and index finger as if she has found a talisman. Abruptly aware of our presence, she stops. We greet her in English. Taken aback, she puts down her bucket and runs off. A few minutes later, a man appears. He does not look threatening, but he has the air of someone on his home turf. The distress his daughter has suffered could be regarded as a form of aggression. His expression is meant to be impassive, and no doubt he thinks that it will make us go away.

At that moment I am reminded of the purpose of my trip to Courland: I must go back with a theme for Henri. By giving me carte blanche, he was handing me a poisoned chalice.

Supposing I chose Louis XVIII's exile at Mitau . . . It is a subject I know quite a lot about. A foretaste of Napoleon on Saint Helena. Louis, in fact, was the first of his kind. In far-distant Courland, penniless, accompanied by a few courtiers who, like those at Longwood, spent their time aping the etiquette of the Tuileries, the king-without-a-kingdom fretted away for far longer than did Napoleon on his rock in the South Atlantic. Mitau is the only obligatory stop on my agenda.

This journey is in danger of turning into a fiasco. I am faced with a blank, an immense blankness similar to this deserted and wind-swept Courland coast without a single object upon which to fix one's gaze. An image of Ingmar Bergman comes to mind, his hair awry, gloomily pacing the deserted shore of his island of Faro, in the Baltic. Even though the Baltic is an enclosed sea, like the Mediterranean, at the moment it hardly strikes me as being conducive to encounters and exchanges of views. There are no boats, not a single ship on the horizon. And always this dull light above a liquid plain resembling ashes.

Courland is one of the four provinces of Latvia, which gained its independence in 1918. I know very little about Latvia, apart from a few vague impressions gleaned from two books: *A Drama in Livonia*, by Jules Verne, and a crime novel, *Pietr-le-Letton*, by Georges Simenon. Livonia formerly comprised present-day Latvia as well as southern Estonia. Curiously, in Verne's book (published in 1904), there are no Latvians, only local Slavs hostile to the Germano-Baltic element. The story takes place near Riga. A bank employee carrying a large sum of money is murdered in an inn run by a German. Everyone accuses a Slav professor, the only person at the scene apart from the innkeeper. But it is the innkeeper who turns out to be the murderer. The Baltic barons* are hauled over the coals while the Russians have things easy.

Before I left home, I buried myself once more with great pleasure in *Pietr-le-Letton*, which happened to be the first Maigret novel. When Simenon wrote this book in 1929, Latvia had only been in existence for nine years. It is obvious that the author had no clear idea of the country. The hero, Pietr, is not very Latvian, but rather an international crook and native of Pskov, in Russia, who had studied at Tartu, in Estonia. His surname is Johansson, a Scandinavian name with nothing Baltic about it. Maigret had done only minimal research. He describes the 1919 riots in a throwaway manner: "Intellectuals defended the German culture, others the Slav culture, others still the region and the local dialects." He writes of "Latvie" rather than the usual French rendering, "Lettonie". The Baltic background is approximate and reduced to the bare essentials. For those who love Simenon, the interest is obviously elsewhere. Maigret's whole world can already be seen in this first novel. The inspector's bulky appearance, his good-natured drinking – without seeming to do so, he is already boozing fairly seriously. His character is well established.

I feel pleased that Simenon should have initiated the adventures of Jules Maigret with this description of Latvia, however fanciful it may be.

THE LECTURER FROM LIEPAJA

We have arrived at Liepaja, formerly Libau. Roses Square, the heart of the city, is filled with a crowd whose gaze is directed at a stage. Felikss Kigelis, a native son and the major figure in Latvian rock music, has just taken leave of his fans. We have missed him.

Two or three guitarists have taken over the proceedings. The spectators, who are mostly young, arc applauding but without getting overexcited. Their enthusiasm can still be seen on their faces. They chant, leap about and clap, but there is no frenzy. Their applause has to do with a kind of amazement such as I have never seen before in a crowd. It is like a form of loyalty, a profound attachment to a particular kind of music, along with the right to enjoy it and make it available without any fuss. There is something very strange indeed about this appropriation, which has a sort of pagan tranquillity about it, but it probably has to do with the personality of Kigelis, who is also a native of Liepaja, and who is the driving force behind Tumsa (Darkness), Latvia's most famous rock group.

We have a meeting with the Resurrector in the Church of the Holy Trinity. Ever since I arrived in Riga, I have been ringing the number my cousin gave me. The meeting was not easy to arrange.

The Church of the Holy Trinity, in the town centre, is a Rococo-style building with a four-storey bell tower. We wait, sitting in a pale-grey pew decorated with a shell. I am delighted by the harmonious simplicity of the altar, the grace of the curves, the gold that accentuates but

55

never excessively. The representation of the Holy Trinity dominates everything; at its foot a cherub struggles with a globe, attempting to hold it aloft. Close to the altar is a loggia, like a box at the theatre, decorated with trophies in the Italian manner.

Apart from the woman at the entrance, who is selling postcards, we are alone. After ten minutes or so, a man of about sixty, with a mane of white hair, bursts in. The tips of his shirt collar are wearing thin, but there is a certain style to the way he dresses, a withered elegance that makes one think of Pre-Raphaelite paintings because of his slenderness and fierce gaze. This is not how I imagined the Resurrector, but in fact he looks the part: he has an air of elegance and the penetrating eye of a man accustomed to making discoveries.

Having exchanged a few words with the attendant, he walks towards us. I am about to get to my feet when I notice him turning round to look behind him. He gazes at the organ for some time. It is a magnificent instrument: the casing and the pipes arranged in clusters in the purest Baroque style are in contrast to the Lutheran starkness of the church.

I soon realize that this is not the man we are expecting. He is the church organist. Before playing it, he admires his instrument. This is probably a ritual. A few minutes later, the sounds of bellows and of stops being pulled out break the silence. I think I recognize Liszt's *Tu es Petrus*. The music almost makes me forget about the Resurrector. The organist then plays some Bach toccatas.

The time of our appointment has passed long since. The man is not going to come. For the moment, I interpret the problems he mentioned on the phone as an excuse for evasiveness. I may be mistaken. In fact he was very busy, his work interrupted by unforeseen events. Furthermore, it was impossible for him to contact me by telephone.

"It's not the end of the world. You haven't come to Courland just to see this guy."

Joëlle is right, but the story about graves and Alsatian soldiers in the Courland Pocket could have made an interesting jumping-off point. I emerge from the church feeling a bit disappointed. An old man is standing at the entrance, beside a statue whose features have been worn away by the elements. I smile at him. He regards me with an irritated expression and walks away.

We are staying in the town centre in a Soviet-style hotel. If one does not take it too seriously, it is not lacking in charm. It is even astonishing. The 1970s architecture looks so shabby and desperately outmoded now that it would be criminal to destroy such a relic. The overall effect is hard to define: a mixture of pseudo-innovation and supposedly modern tubular shapes that were immediately outdated. A good example of ersatz culture. You sense that the Soviet regime was attempting to copy the West to the letter by introducing pseudo-functionalism, a vaguely modular environment inspired by the conquest of outer space. The concrete pillars are bare and eroded; the rendering has become detached from its support. These undulating shapes have become terribly old-fashioned at home, too.

A portly woman stands behind the reception desk. The car park attendant is a witch who has made us park our valiant Skoda in an impossible spot and told us not to move it until we leave. I love the mauve acrylic curtain that divides our bedroom from the bathroom. Pulling down one of the blinds, I knock the holding rail, causing the whole thing to collapse. The tap in the washbasin also activates the shower head.

After a few days, we begin to find this ugliness and lack of comfort pleasant and even grow used to it. It strikes us as the last word in disorientation. The surly woman at reception turns out to be very attentive. All misunderstandings stem from the manner in which one makes oneself understood. Let us not even mention French – a Latvian who knows our language is a rare bird – or elementary English, which a very few people, generally the young, can mumble. The language obstacle is going to be a strain throughout this journey. At the same time, the virtual impossibility of communicating through words will prove productive in the long run. Sign language and mimicry amuse and elicit a smile from the person one is addressing, particularly in a country where the inhabitants are naturally reserved and barricade themselves away from any intrusions. Incapable of making the first step, they are nevertheless delighted to see the foreigner take the initiative. Their defences crumble immediately.

In the evening, in our decrepit bedroom, we read the novels of Eduard von Keyserling. I have brought along ten or so; the books are short and don't take up too much space. This author who wrote in German, and who was born in Courland in the mid-nineteenth century, describes the declining world of the Baltic barons before the cataclysm of 1914. The plots generally unfold in dilapidated mansions where disillusioned, highly sophisticated characters immerse them-selves in conversation and light-hearted banter. They are delightfully decadent but above all extremely ironic. Keyserling makes fun of his characters, but he is not averse to them. On the contrary, he is so fond of them that at times he can appear complacent. The wit derives from this apparent indulgence, which is actually a subtle, almost indiscernible mockery. For Thomas Mann, Keyserling was a role model, the "master of German impressionism", but what consti-tutes "German impressionism" in a literary sense?

I am due to make the acquaintance of Gwenaëlle K., a lecturer in

French at the Liepaja Academy. I have been given her contact details by the cultural office in Riga. Over the telephone, she made it clear that she could not give me much time. Exams were over and she was packing her bags. Even though her "How may I help?" was sweetly expressed, I discerned a note of indifference, something mechanical and, to be honest, disagreeable. The meeting, I fear, will be brief, but I make it a point of principle not to disregard any lead.

We have arranged to meet in a café not far from the canal, a zone that was out of bounds during the Soviet period. There are customers sitting at three tables: a man on his own wearing a leather cap, a silent couple looking at one another without any affection, and a young woman reading a book. It would appear that the establishment has not long been open. The old order, with its cheap statuettes, fake Boukhara carpet and good-natured inanity, exists side by side with the new emblems of consumer society: the pyramid of Coca-Cola stacked on the bar, posters for westerns and the sound of techno music in the background.

My lecturer is beginning to be seriously late. I would be happy to make the acquaintance of the young woman immersed in her book. I admire her delicate neck, her well-defined face, her long, slender legs. Everything about her exudes a certain finesse. She has some slightly snooty mannerisms, of course. She is peering down at her book, but I think this is pure affectation – she does not wish to wear spectacles. I watch her closely, particularly since she cannot see that I am observing her.

When the silent couple are not gazing into their beer glasses, they are glaring at one another. It is as if they are engaged in a mutual loathing competition to see who can outstare the other.

I admire the leather cap worn by the man on his own. It is not actually made of leather but of plastic (the reflections are too bright).

This is the utilitarian socialist headgear with ear-flaps long worn in Communist countries.

Getting to her feet, the young woman looks me over: "I'm Gwenaëlle K. I'm terribly sorry to have kept you waiting. I didn't notice the time; I haven't got a watch."

It is an odd way to introduce oneself. She has some nerve, I think; she knew very well that I was waiting for her. Had she not turned round and looked at me when I'd first come in?

In any case, she does not appear to be the least bit embarrassed. She asks what has brought me to Courland. I tell her that I am not sure myself. She frowns; she probably thinks that I am putting on airs. I could tell her about the article I have been commissioned to write, but that is not the real reason, and, in any case, I do not want to give her complicated explanations.

It is my turn to grill her. She responds with enthusiasm. She arrived in Liepaja ten months ago: "Believe me, it's a complete and utter change of surroundings."

Why does she use that second adjective? She is putting on airs.

"You'll have to forgive me. I've been through a great deal. I didn't know a soul when I got here. Have you seen the place? When I arrived, I was given a flat that went with the job in a totally depressing wreck of a Bolshevik-style building. There was no lock on the front door; I had to buy a chain and padlock. I was within an inch of giving up. But you know, I'm a girl with principles. To have left would have been like abandoning ship. I've kept going and I don't regret it. Believe it or not, I'm now sad to be leaving Liepaja."

She comes from the Atlantic coast of Brittany; she learned Latvian in her spare time.

"It's a strange language. The people are very fond of it. It belongs to the oldest Baltic branch of the Indo-European group. There are no articles. Once you have understood the system of six declensions, it's easy. There's been very little corruption; because of this, Latvian is studied by linguists as a remarkable trace of the original Indo-European way of speaking. In any case, I had no choice: either I shut myself away, or I engaged with people. Here, you don't make the first move, or, more precisely, you don't dare to. The Courlanders are unrefined and a bit uptight. They like comparing themselves to stones: they take a long time to warm up, but once the heat has accrued, it remains."

I imagine that with her very Parisian appearance she must have wrought havoc in Liepaja. I study her face. Her green eyes are hard, yet not without a certain anxiety. Her slightly retroussé nose is narrow and finely delineated. Its distinct shape emphasizes the sternness of her eyes and mouth. She adopts a careful, self-assured air when listening. This expression softens an attitude one might find tedious were it not for the flicker of anxiety that clouds it from time to time. Her charm comes from this blend of fragility and indifference or, more precisely, detachment, which, paradoxically, is not affected. Her refusal to make use of it does not mean that she is unaware of the contradiction, however.

It's hard to question her about her leisure activities in Liepaja except in a vague way. "I suppose you want to know whether my Latvian has stood me in good stead. Yes, it has. In particular, it has helped me to grind flax. Linen is a plant, you know; you have to crush the stalks to separate the fibres."

"Do you mean to say that you have spent your time here weaving linen?"

"No, that's not what grinding flax involves. Besides, it's just an image. I simply meant to say that linen has kept me very busy. Linen

61

is fascinating. It has remarkable dynamometric resistance. It's not used just to make sheets, table linen or clothing, but also tarpaulins and awnings. You're thinking this is just a whim," she added. "Linen has supported Brittany's economy for a long time. It even brought a degree of wealth under the *Ancien Régime*. But they needed to import the seeds. You'll never guess where these seeds came from."

"Courland."

"How did you know?"

"It wasn't difficult to figure out, given the way you phrased the question. Where in Brittany was this flax unloaded?"

"At Roscoff or St Malo. It took three months to sail from Liepaja – or rather Libau."

I do not really understand why the Bretons needed seeds from Courland when they themselves grew flax. Gwenaëlle K. explains that flax seed degenerates very quickly and that it is not possible to use it more than two or three times.

"Don't judge Liepaja on appearances. It doesn't look much at first glance, but you find yourself being won over by its charms. It takes time, I admit. Unfortunately, there's nothing left of its Hanseatic past. If you like, we can take a stroll round the town; it won't take long."

I couldn't have asked for more. She called for the bill in Latvian; she seemed to know the language well.

GWENAËLLE K.

Liepaja is situated on a spit of sand between the sea and a lake, at the mouth of the River Liepa. Gwenaëlle K. offers to show me the harbour.

"Not a very impressive port, I grant you. But it has loads of history. It was from these docks that the Russian fleet embarked for Japan in 1904. It took over seven months to reach the Korea Strait. A real epic voyage, and a tragedy. The Japanese, under the command of Admiral Togo, were waiting at Tsushima. Despite the heroism of the Russians, it was a terrible defeat. The people of Libau have always had close ties to their navy. It was a traumatic moment when the disaster was announced. Disturbances broke out. This is a troubled city; these days, rock music channels its violence. We can scarcely imagine what a tragedy the destruction of her navy was for Russia. It all began at this very spot, on the shores of Courland."

The lecturer in French from Liepaja had found my weak spot: the trace, the mark left by events. Such signs affect me even more when they have become invisible. She describes the departure of the Second Squadron, the first having been destroyed at Port Arthur: "Defeat was on the cards right from the beginning. The Baltic fleet was made up of old, slow-moving warships. There was no preparation. For the crews it was an ordeal right up to the final tragedy. Yet the Russian navy was not lacking in style! I suggest you go to Karosta, where the general staff had their headquarters. The buildings are imposing, though totally in ruins. Karosta, like Liepaja, was out of bounds to foreigners during

63

the Soviet era. Karosta was the largest submarine base in the USSR."

How is one to describe this city without lapsing into clichés about post-Soviet malaise? The streaks of rust on the façades of public buildings – grime resulting from the bad weather – probably existed under Communism. The autocratic town plan seems rooted for all eternity. Lifeless shop windows, pot-holed roads . . . can nothing have changed? In fact, the centre of gravity has shifted imperceptibly. This can be seen in the difference between what remains and what is planned. The sense of heaviness has lessened. Gwenaëlle K. says, "The town centre has changed. For some time now, people have felt the attraction of the sea and the canal."

But the impression of escheatment is deceptive. Signs of rebirth are not yet visible, as if, having hibernated for a long time, the inhabitants are timidly retaking possession of their port, their gardens and their churches.

As far as the lecturer walking just ahead of me is concerned, my feelings border on admiration. If you think about it, it is no small thing to have lived here for ten months having arrived not knowing a soul. Most surprising of all is the ease she radiates. She seems to have adapted to this city without any difficulty.

When she nodded to three or four people whom we encountered on our walk, they greeted her enthusiastically.

"Do you like Cendrars?"* she asks out of the blue. I reply that I do. Perhaps I am too blunt. I imagine that she would have liked me to recite a few verses from *La Prose du Transsibérien*, or to have said something like, "How could one not admire such a free-wheeling traveller who lived at a frenetic pace and, what's more, invented modern poetry?" Yes, I could well have said that, but I did not feel like doing so, possibly because I am impressed by the authority Gwenaëlle K. exerts over this uncertain city.

"Look at these huge sheds. Cendrars' first transatlantic voyage began there; he left for New York from this pier in 1911. It was the main port of departure for emigrants sailing to the United States, the exit gate for the rogues, ragamuffins and downtrodden of the Empire. The majority of Russian Jews who fled the pogroms left from Liepaja. Many of them settled in New York. From 1906 to 1914, there was a weekly sailing, with an average of 80,000 passengers a year. Liepaja was Russian, don't forget, and Cendrars had already made two visits to Russia. *Les Pâques à New York* derived from this journey."

A gust of wind causes some sash windows to rattle. Liepaja's anthem calls it "the city where the wind is born". We walk past the Church of the Holy Trinity, where the Resurrector stood us up. I ask Gwenaëlle K. whether she has heard of this character.

"The Resurrector! Who made that up? You're not serious! Though I do know of a man from Alsace who pays regular visits to Courland to identify the graves of German soldiers. There's talk of gathering them together in a military cemetery."

However much I assure her that "Resurrector" is actually his job title, she makes fun of me. I point out that there is nothing unusual about the word *resurrector*. Originally it designated the motion of getting up from one's seat: "You're wrong to think of him as some sort of miracle worker; you could just as well call him 'The Elevator'." She does not seem convinced: "Why have you come here? To search for this man, or to write about Courland? No need to reply; you'll say, 'Both.' But I'm not sure that a guy who goes around looking for the graves of German soldiers is likely to interest readers of a travel magazine. As for Courland, you only have to look around you. What can you glean from a region that has been losing its identity since 1945? Courland doesn't exist any more. Communism eradicated all of its distinctive features. I should know: since I've been living in Liepaja, I've never heard anyone claim to be a Courlander. We may regret it, but this city and country do not suffer from historical neurosis. The Nazi occupation is never mentioned. The Jewish community was completely decimated with the help of the local population."* She turns towards me. "All the same, you're incredible: you just turn up, hoping to give an identity to a country that's ceased to exist. It's you who are Courland's Resurrector! It's not surprising that this story about vanished graves should appeal to you."

On the main street, where the wind is blowing the dust, she points out a statue.

"Mercury, the god of travellers. You'll need his help, I think. He is also the god of luck, which you will also need."

This Mercury strikes a self-satisfied pose, looking a bit as if he wants to seduce the passers-by. His sandals are adorned with two little wings, but he has lost the caduceus around which, traditionally, two snakes entwine themselves. The manner in which he clenches his empty fist is comical.

"You ought to read some Parquet. He was a lieutenant-colonel who arrived in Libau in 1919 at the head of a French mission. The French are not unknown here. At the time, the port we just saw was filled with French, German and American warships. It was a very unsettled period: even though the First World War was over in the West, Courland was still in a state of great turmoil. As were Estonia and Lithuania, regions which, as you know, had also formed part of Russia before 1914. The Bolshevik armies, the German commandos, the White Russians, not to mention the Latvian troops, were all fighting one another. If you want to understand Courland, you should study that period of the Germano-Baltic barons and the Baltikum. Marguerite Yourcenar describes the atmosphere of that period in *Coup de grâce*. You may not

66

have noticed, but Courland is full of palaces and manor houses. They were the residences of the descendants of the Teutonic Knights. They lost everything in 1920."

Palaces and manor houses: precisely what Henri is interested in. I see the allusion to Yourcenar as a sign. *Coup de grâce* takes me back thirty years to my affair with Mara. She loathed the Baltic barons. Unwittingly, Gwenaëlle K. has propelled me into the past, which, curiously, no longer obsesses me. Since my arrival, I have managed to forget Mara, yet this journey originated with her. Besides, *forget* is not the right word: Mara is like a scar for which there never was a wound. A barely visible sign, a pleasant stigma of the past. Though I rarely think about it, this mark is imprinted on me forever. Occasionally I brush against it and it reminds me of my memories.

Stendhal, whom Mara liked so much, maintains that we travel to rediscover lost sensations, like "the details of hands being clasped in the night". That may be what I am searching for subconsciously: the memory of our hands intertwined and caressing on the staircase of my apartment building in Montreal. This same Stendhal wholeheartedly embraced such foolish notions (in his day, which was much more romantic than our own, it was easier to do so, of course). He added, "I should almost like to become a dupe and halfwit in the reality of life once more, and resume the delightful and utterly preposterous delusions that caused me to do such foolish things."

This is the first time since I arrived in Courland that the obvious thought has sunk in: this is Mara's country. Why has the fact not dawned on me until now? So far, I have been unable to determine a link between her and this elusive place.

I'd forgotten *Coup de grâce* – my Yourcenar period is long past. On the other hand, I consider the film based on it by Volker Schlöndorff to be a masterpiece. It has a mournful charm: winter, snow, a Courland manor house overrun by Bolsheviks, the characters behind closed doors. Watching one of the heroes casually break the ice from a water jug in order to wash himself makes one's teeth chatter. An icy north wind, probably the breath of death, blows through this story at the end of which the heroine, played by Margarethe von Trotta, is shot by the man she loves. This execution scene, which takes place in a railway station in the middle of nowhere, is absolutely chilling. Eric von Lhomond has to fire twice as he turns his head away. Yourcenar wanted this character to represent one of those soldiers of fortune "in the service of all the half-lost or half-won causes". We come across such characters who have lost their way during the brutal crushing of the Spartacist movements, in Germany, in the Manchurian war, in Spain under Franco and, of course, alongside Hitler when he is seizing power.

On my return to Paris, I shall read some Parquet and reread Yourcenar.

We encounter a man wearing a long raincoat. He greets Gwenaëlle K. formally.

"Do you want to know how they look at a Frenchwoman here? Well, they don't look at her, which doesn't mean to say that they don't eye her up, but they do so discreetly, on the sly, while she is looking elsewhere. That's the great difference from France, where they ogle women more or less insistently, depending on how eager or well-mannered they are. Here, they never even exchange glances. In the beginning, I found this strange. I felt as if I were transparent, as if I didn't exist. But one gets used to it very quickly, and in fact it's quite pleasant. There's an outward seriousness here, but it's only a façade. Once the ice is broken, people can be real devils. At weekends the rock-music bars are packed. Liepaja's nickname is 'Liverpool-on-the-Baltic'!"

I don't feel I can ask her anything more about the Courlanders. After all, she has opened up beyond my expectations. Perhaps this is her way of saying that she's told me enough and I shouldn't ask her anything else.

The way she walks differs greatly from the women we pass in the street: the roll of her shoulders, the sway of her hips, the smoothness of her stride as she steps lightly over the ground: there is something unerring and casual about it. A poise and dignity free of any heaviness. There is less pride and more freedom in the gait of Latvian women, but, paradoxically, this spontaneity makes them look more affected. They stroll along naturally, as if unaware of the glances of the men who, according to Gwenaëlle K., do not stare at women.

We have reached my hotel, whose renovated architecture has aged so poorly – the rendering that has come away from its support gives it an honourably decayed aspect. The building, which cannot be more than thirty years old, is clearly on its last legs. But time's depredations have been curbed, the disintegration narrowly halted by building works: holes filled in, the roughcast of the façade crudely applied and reworked in a glossy grey, the entrance hall touched up. This artificial restoration touches me deeply. My socialist hotel had been within a hair's breadth of collapsing, but, as it happens, it has not fallen down. It hangs on, head into the wind.

"Is your hotel all right?"

"Not bad at all. I would even say I'm becoming increasingly fond of it."

"Well, I must leave you. I've suggested a few leads for you to follow up. Now it's over to you. Good luck!"

She shook my hand and smiled. I watched her walk away, disappear round the corner. She turned to wave before she was swallowed up by the wind. In novels, at moments like this, the narrator or hero thinks to himself, 'Curious person, striking, magnetic even. And to think that I shall never see her again . . .' No need to point out that he will, of course. But nothing of the sort happens in Liepaja. Gwenaëlle K., the authority on linen, vanished from my life for ever, a brief apparition who opened a few perspectives for me.

I tell Joëlle about my encounter. She is sorry not to have met the lecturer and informs me that Henri has been trying to reach me. I must ring him back.

I find my friend in laconic form, precise, very much the professional: "It's all go here." He wants to know where I am. My vague replies annoy him.

"What have you got for me? Specifically, I mean. You mentioned manor houses. Have you visited any – even one?"

"Not yet. But they are everywhere."

"What are they like?"

"I told you, I haven't seen any yet."

"But you've just told me that they're everywhere. Please don't let me down!"

What is the matter with him? He is getting het up about my article. He must think that I'm not getting out enough. He has changed: in Paris he confided in me and made no particular demands. "Freestyle stuff" was what he asked for. I had even thought that he took me for some sort of artistic skater, which, on reflection, was not such a silly idea. I have a tendency to glide and wend my way round obstacles. Sometimes, I also come a cropper.

Henri is not entirely wrong to be anxious. For the time being, it is clear that Courland is evading, even alarming, me. I can't grab hold of it; it's impossible to make the connection between its rich history and

70

the present day, which strikes me as drab and colourless. "A traveller should have the courtesy to give himself an aim as he travels", Stendhal observes in his *Journal*. I must be an ill-mannered traveller, lacking an objective or genuine determination, a wandering boor, travelling for the sake of revelation, disclosure or self-realization. I have never believed in this sort of nonsense. One does not visit a foreign land in order to know oneself but rather, in theory anyway, to search out the unknown, to experience other people.

In any case, reading Keyserling's novels has provided me with little information about Courland. I have just finished *Versant sud.** Apart from the avenues of lime trees, the mansions and the Germanic names, the author does not describe the local colour. The end-of-the-world atmosphere is well depicted, however. You sense that these highly civilized country squires are enjoying the gentle pleasures of a life that will soon come to an end. They are hurtling towards catastrophe, and they know it. An inevitable mood of disaster haunts these disillusioned individuals.

THE POLYTONAL ROCKER

Partially sunk wrecks lie offshore, their hulls protruding above the water. A few kilometres to the north of Liepaja, Karosta was the Soviet Empire's second naval base, numbering 26,000 men. Before leaving Courland in 1994, the Russians chose to scuttle all the ships and submarines that they were unable to take home. Countless warships lie on the sea bottom; it is impossible to know how many. It is even said that nuclear submarines were sunk. Gwenaëlle K. assured me that the sea had become a radioactive dustbin. The seafront, once scattered with fortifications, provides a spectacle of devastation. Casemates, turrets and blockhouses have been demolished but have not disappeared; on the contrary, they are accentuated, severely damaged and mangled, made all the more monstrous by the incompleteness of their destruction. You might think it had been an act of vandalism perpetrated by a race of Cyclops. Reckless ravaging has resulted in a huge amount of daubing on the walls along the shore. One suspects the *acte gratuit*, the impulse to destroy in order to avenge.

Cattle graze among the ruins. Shrubs have succeeded in growing amid the wrecked buildings, which bear traces of graffiti: *no future* or *fuck you*. On a shattered wall, a fresco of striking beauty depicts two hearts joined by a safety pin. What did the anonymous artist intend to express? "Hope!" Joëlle says. "Destroy in order to go on living."

It is hard to imagine that the former headquarters of the Russian navy should lie just two kilometres from Liepaja. Today, Karosta is an

72

enclave cut off from the outside world, further isolated by a swivelling bridge (designed by Gustave Eiffel), a masterpiece of metal architecture.

Dilapidated houses, rows of ransacked buildings. Surrounded by Ladas in the parking lot, our Skoda does not complain: it belongs to the genuine socialist family but with a more brazen aspect, possibly due to its poppy-red paintwork, as shiny as lacquer. From amid the post-Soviet wreckage one marvel emerges: the Orthodox Church of St Nicholas, consecrated in 1903 by Tsar Nicholas II himself. Four secondary onion domes support the central one, a symbol of Christ surrounded by the four Evangelists.

A young man with dirty hair suggests that we have a look at the interior. He does not smile; he offers his services with a certain degree of coldness. Though I refuse, he is persistent and comes into the church with us. We try to avoid him by making our way towards the iconostasis, but he follows us quietly. His lack of emotion and blank expression make us uneasy.

"Before leaving for Japan in 1904, the Russian navy took part in a great ceremony here to beg Our Saviour for help," he declares with icy calm.

It is at that point that I begin to regard this tall devil with his emaciated face and impassive expression rather differently. The Russo-Japanese War was an extraordinary event. The Empire of the Rising Sun, which, less than forty years earlier, had still been stuck in the Middle Ages, inflicted an overwhelming defeat on one of the major Western powers. It was the end of a world, the twilight of the white man's supremacy, the culmination of the tsarist regime. The revolts and mutinies that followed the rout were precursors of the 1917 Revolution. Indeed, it was at Karosta that it all began.

"Are you Russian?"

73

"My family comes from Novgorod, but I've always lived here. I don't know Russia."

The church smells of incense, worn-out carpets and old fur. For Western Europeans accustomed to silent, deserted sanctuaries, it is always astonishing to step inside an Orthodox church. Energy and intensity are immediately apparent. The icons, their contrasting colours emerging from the darkness, are imbued with an impetuosity that transfigures the space. These figures from the Old and New Testaments may be static and the basilica poorly lit, yet one senses an intimate familiarity with the Deity.

A dozen or so babushkas are gathered round the priest, singing at the tops of their voices as he swings a censer with a fervour that lends the scene an almost barbaric feeling. A sense of urgency pervades the ceremony even though one can see perfectly well that the old women have all the time in the world.

"Coming to this church is the only thing that makes life bearable for these poor women. They don't speak a word of Latvian."

The young man explains that, before granting naturalization to new immigrants, the state imposes humiliating tests in Latvian language and history. Although his expression is still surly, he has realized that he can easily sway me by martialling historical references. Joëlle, who has seen through his game, whispers, "He's starting to get on my nerves." We try to lose him.

"Wait, wait, Monsieur! Don't go. Listen to me! Karosta is dying. Look at what they have done to Karosta . . ."

Despite the force of his remarks, the young man's sharp-featured face remains impassive. Nevertheless he gestures charmingly, inviting us to return to the iconostasis. The old women continue to chant, their expressions suffused with gentleness, as if their earlier trance has

74

soothed them. The priest has stopped swinging the censer. He more and more resembles the transfigured icon of the Holy Countenance behind him. His chubby face is simultaneously affectionate and radiant. Hovering in the air is the somewhat sickly smell of spices and the reek of stale sweat.

"We were invincible!" the young man says without our knowing what he is alluding to.

He explains that the church was damaged during the First World War and then closed by the Soviets during their first occupation – he does not use the word *occupation*, of course. After the Nazi invasion in 1941, soldiers from the anti-aircraft defence moved into the building. After the war, it was used as a warehouse by the Soviet military, then as a naval club.

When travelling, one is often hampered by ignorance. One can only rely on chance for assistance, or on the kindness of strangers like this Russian. Stendhal is a good example. Now there was a man who never compelled anyone or forced the hand of destiny! His one rule was to encourage people to speak with him about what they knew best. He did not conceal the fact that this was a selfish pleasure. Above all, being a free spirit, his aim was not to state what things were but to "describe the effect they had on him".

Our clinging companion's name is Vladimir. He tells us that he is a member of a rock group of the "total polytonal variety", complete with hooter, siren and "Chinese hat" (a cone-shaped percussion instrument complete with small bells). This is clearly a subject that means a great deal to him. In accordance with Stendhal's precepts, I let him speak about his passion. He is apparently the group's lead singer. He writes the lyrics: "It's easy. It's all in the leitmotif. You introduce the theme, you speak it, and then you keep on repeating what you've just said over

75

and over again. It's the same in politics. Except that in our case, we sing."

I suggest that we continue our conversation outside the sanctuary.

"Why bother? It's seen a lot, this church! My dream is to give a rock concert here, but the Orthodox clergy are not ready for that sort of event." His expression becomes animated and he seems more at ease. "The sound in Liepaja is unique. It's to do with the humidity, the wind, the Baltic, with our position between the sea and the lake. Perhaps also with our having been an enclosed city for so long." I give up trying to understand his explanations about polytonal rock. He persists: "It's very simple, Monsieur. Wagner uses polytonality in *Tristan und Isolde*. Just as Darius Milhaud does, and as Stravinsky does in *Petrushka*. It accentuates the pathetic and despairing side of our music. But we're not desperate; quite the contrary. We love the present, the here and now, life. And this ruined city makes it all possible!"

Apparently, he sings indiscriminately in Russian, in Latvian and in English, of course. The other members of the group are Latvian. Throughout the Baltic, Liepaja has been famous for many years for its rock festivals, which were tolerated even in Soviet times. Latvians are crazy about the group that calls itself Tumsa, a musicians' initiative that originated in Liepaja.

He is hard to pin down, this Vladimir. He is both nostalgic for former Russian glory and a foreigner in the country in which he lives without ever having known any other. Yet he is not unhappy to have become a Latvian citizen: "In December 1991, I participated in the first Orthodox liturgical ceremony since independence. Afterwards, everything happened very quickly. The last Russian servicemen left Karosta in 1994." The proclamation of independence did not bother Vladimir. The only thing that annoyed him was the status of non-citizens, referred to as "grey passports". Ever since the Soviet Union ceased to exist, these Russian-speakers have had no nationality. Yet 35 per cent of the Latvian population speaks Russian as its native tongue.

Vladimir suggests that we leave the basilica and visit the disused military camp. The place looks more like a residential district than a billet. The streets are dead straight. Each block contains buildings that are veritable palaces. These sumptuous structures, adorned with colonnades and furnished with huge terraces and loggias, date from the reigns of Alexander III and Nicholas II. They were built in a pastiche of designs suggesting Rome, the Renaissance, Palladio and the embellishments of Haussmann, a mixture of the Musée d'Orsay and the palaces of St Petersburg. The spirit of ancient Russia, with its history of disaster, disturbance and suffering, hangs over the desolate camp.

"What utter decadence!" Vladimir keeps on exclaiming. The surroundings symbolize an aspect of Russia's unfathomable mystery, the "flight to disaster" that Georges Nivat has examined in detail.* "We Russians are nomads. No-one understands us. My parents wound up here; I didn't choose the place. By birth, I am an ambiguous (he uses the English word) man: Slav, probably European. Latvian . . . I still don't know what that is."

Russian families squatting in some of the buildings have used rags to block up the windows. Large cans of water, bicycles and motorbikes are piled in the hallways, which are decorated with plant motifs (grape clusters, roses, acanthus leaves). Only the former headquarters of the officers of the tsarist navy have been spared. There we encounter men in uniforms and white caps: cadets in the new Latvian navy. They are trained in this palace, which, on closer inspection, is also fairly dilapidated. But this is deceptive. Shoddily patched up, it retains signs of its former glory.

The place is unlike anything we have ever experienced. It is a dead town, a sort of luxury suburb abandoned at the planning stage. The feeling of space is accentuated by the vast, unenclosed parkland surrounding the buildings. This town created by the tsars does not belong to any known category of urban planning. Nevertheless, the buildings have a faintly familiar sophistication even though the area has the curious feel of a wasteland. It is pre-1917 Russia, a vaguely Westernized lost paradise, a Chekhovian illusion constructed on the shores of the Baltic Sea, on land that is not Russian but Baltic. What is "Baltitude"? It is too soon to answer that question. I try to quiz my Russo-Latvian friend on the matter. "Firstly, it's a negation. 'Baltic' is neither Russian, nor German, nor Scandinavian." I observe that identity should not be defined exclusively in negative terms, a point he accepts as he starts humming to himself.

We say "Baltic states" for convenience. Estonia, Latvia and Lithuania have shared a common fate – Soviet occupation – but nowadays each of them is trying to play its own role.

It suddenly occurs to me that there is an extraordinary freshness about this country. It has none of the picturesque characteristics we are accustomed to when we visit Italy, Spain, Holland, England or Germany. It is not a land of dreams: no elements of fantasy, no eccentricities, no preconceived notions affect this part of Europe. Yet one does not feel totally disorientated. The eye can be trained; it can discern signs that are not totally foreign. To be Baltic is perhaps a way of slipping into this in-between space. A form of interbreeding. The German, Swedish and Russian invaders gave the place a plural, and conflicting, identity. The laboratory of Europe may well be situated in this forward-looking area where people never stop borrowing from others in order to create an identity for themselves, a character so original that everyone overlooks it. To be a Courlander, on the other hand, is another matter. And here I am ill-equipped, to say the least. What does my polytonal rocker really think of Courland? It is his country, after all: was he not born in Karosta?

"It is like amber. Solid, hard, smooth in appearance. You think you can see through it, but that's an illusion. You know, amber is able to alter its shape. Watch out, Monsieur, for Courland and its unreality! When you rub amber on a bit of fabric, it has the power to attract lighter substances. You have succumbed to the appeal of a name. But you have to be strong to resist Courland."

Vladimir must take me for a simpleton. Amber is big business on the Baltic Sea. This much sought-after bituminous substance is a resinous fossil. One finds small or large fragments of it thrown up by the sea. Vladimir points out that the Latvians' name for the Baltic is *Dzintarjura*, "the amber sea".

"At home in France, we say 'sharp as amber' to describe someone who is astute."

"Courlanders have other attributes that come more readily to mind. They are compact, square in shape and rather inflexible."

"Do you really believe in those ethnological characteristics, Vladimir? Surely they are mere inventions and we continue to use them out of habit and laziness."

"Oh, they do exist, but I agree: they are somewhat made up. People are frightened of vagueness. It reassures them to believe that they themselves possess attributes of the land in which they were born."

We are walking through the ruins of Karosta. Curiously, the grass that surrounds the dilapidated buildings has been mown. There is a striking contrast between what looks like an English lawn – yellowed, it is true, by the sun – and this desolation in which time's destructive power is conspicuous. Might it be the new state's intention to allow the site, a symbol of the Russian and – later – the Soviet yoke to wither and die?

"No, no, it's much simpler than that. It is *too late*. You appear to like the past, Monsieur, but it can never be reincarnated. It's the opposite with rock music: we live in an eternal present; we don't carry the past around with us. The impossibility of getting rid of oneself, that's the problem for human beings today. Rock has solved this problem."

He seems very sure of himself, our cicerone. Evidently he thinks of memory as regression. I wonder what he would think of a mission like that of the Resurrector, a man who exhumes the remains of Wehrmacht soldiers. To my astonishment, Vladimir has heard of this character, has recently read an article about him. "What's the point of digging up those fascists?" he says. *Fascist* is the word the Soviets used to designate the Nazis, the term they employed, in fact, for all Germans. I point out that it is mainly a matter of identifying the dead, not such a contemptible thing. "We destroyed their graves after the war, probably in order to try and forget the horror," he says. I reply that this argument is a bit facile: "Many of those German soldiers can be thought of as victims. For example, there were Alsatians who were dragooned into the Wehrmacht. Was it necessary to make them die a second death by desecrating their graves?" I try to explain the history of the *malgré-nous*; Vladimir does not wish to understand. He considers them collaborators.

On the outskirts of the residential area loom buildings constructed in the purest Soviet style. Erected in the 1970s, these endlessly patched-up apartment blocks bear witness to the desperate poverty and resourcefulness of the Russian people. There is a naked truth here that they do not attempt to conceal. The tangled mass of electric wires, the thick grime deposited on the exteriors by the bad weather, the flaking walls – these are all exposed, out in the open. That is the essence of modernity: strip it bare, expose the mechanism. The very opposite of decoration.

We come across another hidden aspect of Karosta. A vast red-brick building looms in front of us, causing Vladimir some embarrassment. He would like us to disregard it. Intrigued, I question him. Eventually he tells us that it is the former military prison. Tourists are invited here to re-enact the Soviet era in what is described as an "extreme experience". For the equivalent of ten euros, you can spend a night in a damp, icy cell, plunged in darkness. A K.G.B. officer barks out orders and prevents you from sleeping. The prisoner is obliged to do gymnastics in order to keep warm and must empty the toilets with a spoon. You can also be a spectator at the "execution" of an inmate found guilty of trying to escape. No detail is omitted: the show ends with a shot being fired and an agonizing, formal silence. "You are now leaving Hell", a slogan assures you.

Vladimir prefers to take us down a grand avenue that leads towards the sea. Dating from the time of Nicholas II, it is paved entirely with marble – "Finnish marble," Vladimir specifies, not without pride. The slabs have deteriorated and are coming apart; their surfaces are strewn with numerous cracks that glitter in the sunlight. In my opinion, they are not made of marble but of red porphyry, recognizable from the little white marks that are feldspar crystals. But what is the point of showing off my knowledge? In any case, I don't know the English word. As to this sloping causeway, Vladimir tells me a mind-boggling story about priests blessing the imperial ships as they set sail for faraway destinations. I know this is incorrect, that it is an invention intended to curry favour with me, which is not difficult. He does not even try to deceive me. It is a way of testing me: he has understood my obsession, my fascination with the incredible adventure that was the voyage of the Second Pacific Squadron, departing from these shores to take control of the Sea of Japan.

"We lost because we no longer believed in ourselves," Vladimir says. Now he is playing the role of imprecator. This ability to move from one identity to another exhausts me. Vladimir is a multifaceted person. A nostalgic and critical Soviet, a stateless Russian, a pseudo-Latvian, a wandering Courlander, a non-persecuted dissident, he does not even need to shift from one role to another; he assumes them all at the same time. He suffers from a profound handicap: he does not know who he is.

"Isn't that enough?" Joëlle whispers to me. I get the feeling that she has had her fill of Vladimir. He certainly does exactly as he pleases, and he is a ham actor, to put it mildly. To say that I was beginning to grow fond of him may be an exaggeration, but his unpredictable temperament, his cultural knowledge and his impassive expression appealed to me. Now, he is becoming incoherent. I have the feeling that we will get no further with him.

The traveller is an egotist; as soon as he has exhausted one curiosity, he grows weary and impatient to move on to something else. The author of *Rome, Naples et Florence* describes very well the sense of joy he experienced "every time it was a matter of leaving and seeing new sights". Stendhal may come across as "a sentimental type with a hard-hearted eye", yet I see this highly perceptive man as "a hard-hearted type with a sentimental eye", in fact. He takes his leave ruthlessly. No sooner has the tourist had his fill than he wants to be gone. This urge cannot be controlled.

We set off in the direction of the car. Vladimir follows us half-heartedly. He has understood; he is putting on a brave face. Before leaving us, though, he asks me for a favour: an English–Latvian dictionary. I find this cool way of scrounging amusing. I agree to send him a dictionary once I am back in France. I keep my promise without knowing whether he has received the book or not. One day I am surprised to have him turn up at my home in Paris. You don't get rid of a polytonal rocker all that easily.

THE BATTLE OF TSUSHIMA

It was at Karosta that preparations were made for the great expedition that was to culminate at Tsushima in the Sea of Japan.

On 14 October 1904, the crowds hurried to Libau to cheer Admiral Rozhestvensky and the sailors of the Second Pacific Squadron. There were people everywhere, on the rooftops, in the trees. The tsar, who had come especially from St Petersburg, blessed the fleet. Salutes were fired, and bells were rung.

The superficial elation barely concealed the armada's pitiful state. The ships were defective; revolutionary propaganda meant that the crews were poorly prepared and trained, and the officers full of misgivings. Every day, mysterious problems would arise. Admiral Rozhestvensky, the fleet's commander, knew where he stood when it came to ships and men. Alone in his mansion in Karosta, he had realized that there was no point in patching up the equipment or training the recruits indefinitely. No matter what happened, they were never going to be ready. He was convinced that it was necessary to rig out the ships without delay and head for the open sea in order to extricate himself from the harmful atmosphere being created by the government. Only departure and making for their objective would clear away doubts and instil faith.

There is something of the hero of a Corneille tragedy about Rozhestvensky, a far-sighted, unbending man and a seasoned sailor immured in silent pride. He knows that all is lost. And that he will be blamed. He is not caught between the devil and the deep blue sea, but between disaster foretold and certain disgrace. He knows that he has no room to manoeuvre.

To reach Port Arthur, you had virtually to sail round the world, down the coast of Africa, around the Cape of Good Hope and through the Strait of Malacca, heading for the China Sea. Even the battleships' gallant names had a derisory ring to them: *Souvorov, Alexander III, Borodino*.

Weighing anchor had been disastrous. Because wind had filled the harbour with seaweed and mud, the ships had remained at a standstill for a long time. Such a start did not augur well. There was an incident off Hull when the squadron sank an English fishing boat and damaged two of its own cruisers. They were within a hair's breadth of a confrontation with the Royal Navy, but the unruffled Rozhestvensky sailed on.

The damage to the cruisers meant that the convoy had to keep slowing its speed, and it was necessary to wait for vessels that had been delayed or were equipped with insufficiently powerful engines. The problem for all battleships of this period was their huge consumption of coal. Maintaining fuel supplies for the Second Pacific Squadron provided the admiral with a headache, and the fact that Russia was being treated like a pariah at the time added to the ordeal. The British, in particular, did everything in their power to make life a misery for him. The difficulties began in Vigo, then continued in Dakar. At Libreville, in what was then the French Congo, cargo had to be transferred from one ship to another outside territorial waters. In Portuguese Angola, the squadron was given no more than twenty-four hours to take on fresh supplies. In Madagascar, the admiral was informed of the Russian surrender at Port Arthur. Did his assignment still have a purpose?

The stopover at Nossi-Bé dragged on and on and proved a nightmare. It was thought that the expedition would meet its end on this far-flung island, where problems kept multiplying due to the humidity. A short time later, while still at Nossi-Bé, the fleet heard the news of "Red Sunday".* Hesitating, Rozhestvensky realized that he was irretrievably on his own. The government in St Petersburg was incapable of taking the slightest decision. It fell to him, to him alone, to choose whether to turn back or continue. He decided to carry on, knowing that the epic journey would end in disaster.

Seven and a half months after setting out from Libau, the sacrifice took place in the Korea Strait on 27 May 1905. Admiral Togo had been expecting his victim for a long time. Battle commenced with an extremely audacious manoeuvre by the Japanese, who exposed the fleet to enemy guns for a quarter of an hour without the Russians being able to retaliate. Despite the vastly disproportionate forces, it took over six hours for the Japanese fleet to overcome the Second Pacific Squadron. By this time, due to exercise drill and Rozhestvensky's iron will, his crew had become hardened fighters. Once again, in their misery, the Russians displayed unbelievable courage and tenacity. The tsarist navy had given priority to the recruitment of Courland sailors, renowned for their experience. They fought with exemplary bravery.

Only three ships out of forty-five managed to escape from the trap of Tsushima and reach Vladivostok. Over 5,000 Russian sailors perished, and more than 6,000 were captured, among them Rozhestvensky. The Japanese suffered only a hundred or so losses.

The government in St Petersburg later sought to persuade the admiral that he had been betrayed. He loftily dismissed the idea, just as he refused to blame his defeat on the technical inferiority of his fleet. He accepted total responsibility with an admirable sense of abnegation and duty.

Karosta–Tsushima: today we cannot conceive how indissolubly

linked these two names are. The expression "the Yellow Peril" dates from this period. After Red Sunday, the second fateful blow to the tsarist regime would fall within the poisoned confines of Courland's naval headquarters, the symbol of its lack of preparation. The shock wave spread as far as the two islands between Korea and Japan, and back again to Libau, where news of the disaster would provoke an uprising that would spread like wildfire throughout Russia.

For the Japanese empire, the achievement of Tsushima paved the way for an era of success and conquest that would result in an expansionist political policy, ultimately culminating in Pearl Harbor. "In this sense", wrote Frédéric Rousseau,* "Tsushima may be seen as the monstrous womb of Hiroshima."

Tsushima caused much ink to flow. Jack London, Tolstoy and, in particular, Claude Farrère seized on it. The latter's novel, *La Bataille*, is written from the Japanese point of view. Save for his reflections on a civilization which he idealized, the work is interesting because of its detailed description of the confrontation between the Russians and the Japanese. On board a Japanese battleship there is a British officer. He does not take part in the fighting, but he observes the extraordinary efficiency of the Japanese navy, "a fleet constructed in England, equipped in England, and trained according to English methods and principles". The Russian shells fall short, but one eventually hits the foredeck, "scattering a few corpses here and there". The battle scenes and the death of Marquis Yorisaka Sadao, the ship's commander, are remarkably portrayed. The Japanese officer dies reciting a love poem, helped by the British officer who has absconded with his wife.

MANOR HOUSE OR PALACE?

The park is deserted. Ditches, loose paving stones and rubble litter the pathways and the palace lawn. Not a living soul. At the main gate, the polished red of the Skoda looks rather garish. I park out of sight. In these late June days, the scent of box fills the countryside. Our first Courland palace: Kazdanga. Henri is going to be pleased! Everything fits the dream of a lost country mansion complete with portico, six pillars, triangular pediment and rendering that has fallen off in patches to reveal the brickwork. Exactly the right amount of neglect makes restoration easy to imagine. Unlike Karosta, the situation here is not desperate. The palace probably is inhabited. A basketball pitch in the park makes it clear that Kazdanga has become a school. But there are neither teachers nor pupils.

One of the doors is open. We go in. The hall smells of cabbage and damp. A brochure in Latvian, with a summary in German at the end, has been left out on a sideboard. It gives an account of the estate, which belonged to the Manteuffel family, who lived here from 1533 to 1923. The building was damaged by fire during the peasant uprising of 1905, then restored in 1907. To judge from a nineteenth-century engraving reproduced in the brochure, one could easily mistake the building for an English manor house: a small lake with swans, coppices, horizontal terraces, perfect outlines.

We hear footsteps on the floor above. A man hails us from the top of the staircase. He has removed the headphones of his personal stereo.

He is dressed in an old green T-shirt. Though his voice is loud, his tone is not at all aggressive. Is he aware that these intruders are foreigners? He walks slowly down the stairs, an arrogant expression on his face. He speaks only Latvian. He makes gestures that we do not understand, drawing circles with his right hand, before dropping his arms in a gesture of helplessness. Impossible to communicate with him. He has realized that we are French, or so it would appear. No longer on his guard, he agrees to let us see a large room that is empty except for a vast earthenware stove. Imperial motifs adorn the walls.

An old photograph shows a family in front of the house, probably the Manteuffels. The atmosphere is right out of Keyserling's novels: the last flickers of happiness before tragedy strikes. The mother wears a fine, melancholy expression. Her hair is tied with a ribbon at her neck. The man, who is about fifty, wears a dark jacket and light-coloured trousers. He seems to have a ruddy complexion, unless it is the quality of the print that has darkened his cheeks. His eyes have a genial look. A girl with strong features stares defiantly at the camera; she is wearing a loose-fitting white dress and a beribboned hat. Her face puts me in mind of the puritanical, mystical Emily Dickinson, the poet who chose to shut herself away in a convent.

In what circumstances was the photograph taken? Probably between 1907, the period when the palace was rebuilt, and 1914. The rendering on the façade appears to be new; the house had evidently just been restored. So this was the ancient dwelling of one of the Baltic barons, descendants of the Teutonic Knights and the Livonian Brothers of the Sword who conquered these lands in the Middle Ages. The palace is also known by the German name of Katzdangen.

During the stormy periods experience by the Grand Duchy of Courland – occupied as it was by the Poles, the Swedes and, later, the

Russians – the Germano-Baltic lords knew how to withdraw adroitly. Without any qualms, they transferred their allegiances to the service of the tsarist state, which annexed the duchy in 1795. This new affiliation allowed the large landowners to extend their privileges a bit further over a peasantry long subjected to serfdom and compelled to carry out menial duties up until the mid-nineteenth century. The brutality of Red Sunday, which would be exacerbated by the disaster of Tsushima, spread to all of the Baltic countries. In Courland, nearly 300 estates and mansions were attacked by a rural proletariat up in arms against the latifundia of the aristocrats. For this German-speaking nobility, the peasants' revolt of 1905 was the first warning call before 1914. But few heard it. The 1917 Revolution would represent a point of no return. After Latvian independence, all estates of more than 110 hectares would be nationalized. Most of the Baltic barons would leave the country and seek refuge mainly in Germany, thus bringing eight centuries of supremacy to an end.

The caretaker in the green T-shirt draws our attention to a coat of arms: "Manteifelu, Manteifelu . . ." I can just make out the black eagle of Prussia, a crown and birds' wings at the top of the armorial bearings. The noble families of Germany and central Europe loved to adorn their coats of arms with improbable animal fantasies, often to do with hunting: antlers, boars' heads and the like.

A whiff of charcuterie and disinfectant hangs over the silent, deserted palace. You can tell that it's the long vacation and that the place has only been abandoned temporarily. Life has gone on leave for the summer. The caretaker also seems to have fallen into a state of semi-torpor verging on friendliness, but the language problem is clearly insuperable. Raising his arms in a gesture of helplessness, he points towards the huge trees in the garden as if inviting us to explore it. The park is imposing; later I learn that it is the finest arboretum in Courland. On a mound by one of the paths, we discover a small grave-yard containing eight tombs. A few names are still legible: Caroline von Manteuffel (1800–1830), Mathilde Gräfin Lambsdorff (1819–1839), Lina von Manteuffel (1849–1866).

In Courland, which seems so foreign, whose landscapes and villages are unlike the ones that we know, in this country with no equivalent, I keep trying to identify familiar aspects. The palaces with their estates, certainly; the trees, no doubt: they punctuate space, whether in prox-imity to buildings or spread out around them – we are certainly in Europe. Yet there is a disengagement from time here, an inner quality that I am unable to pinpoint or define. I cannot quite grasp its signifi-cance. I can see the outline but not the core.

I frequently consult my Latvian–French dictionary, but do not easily find words that alter meaning according to their declension. *Pils* is the first Latvian word with which we become familiar. It means "chateau". We often say, "Look, a *pils*!" when we come across a sign at the entrance to a village. The second word we have had to learn is *muiža* (important not to forget the circumflex over the "z"), which may be translated as "estate". On the few signposts and so on where words are translated into English, "manor house" and "palace" are used indiscriminately. Palaces generally have the sense of a castle, whereas manor houses denote large, attractive dwellings intended purely for relaxation and enjoyment. The French language distinguishes badly between these two things. Buildings constructed during the seven-teenth, eighteenth and even the nineteenth centuries correspond to the precise definition of a manor house. There is nothing defensive or lordly about them. Nevertheless, we continue to call them "chateaux".

*

A dusty road leads to Laidi, a house that was probably built at the beginning of the nineteenth century. Situated a few kilometres from Kazdanga, it is fairly attractive, also in the Palladian style. The Ionic columns at the entrance and on the two wings are intended to impart a distinguished air to the ensemble, which is quite simple but harmonious. Part of the roof is covered in asbestos. The syringa in the garden gives off a strong scent. Once again, I am struck by the strangeness of the spectacle. The overall setting of park and house is similar to what we might find at home, but the contours and exterior are very different from anything in France. I believe the dissimilarity is due to the sharpness of the light. It is as if objects were diffusing their own luminous waves.

Courland: a reverse image of Italy. Of course, this is only a phrase. But it is a satisfactory point of departure from which to report on a country that is so *unknowable*, that is – for all the sparseness of its artistic treasures – far from being deprived. The concision of Courland as against the profusion of Italy. It is not quite like the West, but the model is the same. Like our chateaux, these palaces no longer hold sway. Only the villages, with their old Lutheran churches surmounted by square towers, and their single shops and obligatory museums, have life left in them. We are well and truly in a Europe interconnected through its fields, forests and church towers. And its traditions. Yet that devilish business of analogy, which often allows one to extricate oneself from a situation without embarrassment, does not function here.

Almost everyone has been to Italy. People who have never set foot there know it anyway. Not merely through familiar images such as the Leaning Tower of Pisa, the Colosseum or the Grand Canal, but through landscapes dominated by cypress trees, cathedral domes and red-brick palaces.

Tackling Venice, risky subject par excellence, Henry James declares that it is impossible to express anything original about that city. He goes so far as to comment, "There is notoriously nothing more to be said on the subject." You then wonder: after such an introduction, how is he going to extricate himself? Because it is clear that this preamble is announcing his intention to confront the difficulty. He writes further: "It would be a sad day indeed when there should be something new to say." A volte-face? I don't think so. James is making it clear that it can be delightful to discuss hackneyed subjects: we are on well-trodden ground. Venice belongs to the self-evident world of European sensibility. The laboured circumlocutions, the well-worn pronouncements are merely polite gestures. It seems to me that what he is intending to express is that, when all is said and done, one writes in response to a call of duty. Making sure that the legacy is intact, that it continues to affect us. Anything unusual would damage the charm.

Such are the considerations going through my mind as I stand in front of Laidi, admiring the mascarons that decorate the façade. I had not noticed the other visitors. They have just completed their tour and are returning to their car. They are foreigners. The father is about forty. His hair is smoothed with brilliantine and his spectacles have gold rims. A rucksack hangs from his right shoulder. He is wearing a narrow-striped cotton suit and suede tennis shoes. The wife, who is blonde, slightly plump and agile, is calling to the children, who are busy picking wild strawberries. From the parents' expressions, the way they move and their clothing, it is clear that they are not from these parts. When I travel, I amuse myself by trying to place people based on their appearance. Russians, for example, have a much more extrovert way of behaving than Latvians. They speak loudly and are not at all bothered by people looking at them. Their outfits are garish, even ostentatious, whereas Latvians are always appropriately dressed and seem to be constantly on their guard.

These foreigners getting into their car are clearly not Russian. American, possibly? But they don't have the body language, that compact way of holding themselves, of sauntering, of using their hands or, to put it another way, the ostentatious appearance of ease. Frequently the cut of clothing – trousers and shirts especially – gives Americans away. Are these people French? Certainly not. I am sometimes mistaken, but I flatter myself that I recognize my fellow countrymen with ease. It is hard to define Frenchness: a chilly, restless manner, simultaneously disjointed and controlled; a way of puffing out our chests and looking weary. Not everyone is endowed with such contradictory style. French women are identifiable by the way they walk, their technique of commodious sauntering, of strolling. Only they can quicken their pace *slowly, cautiously*, as if they were walking on eggs; only they can swing their hips wearing that hangdog expression that is our national trademark. You have the sense that they have always known they were being scrutinized. Their little game consists of feigning indifference.

I walk over to the car. A German number plate. I would never have guessed.

The first tourists, pioneers like us. How have they come to be here?

Our hotel is a sort of post-Soviet Flatotel in the middle of the countryside. The vast restaurant area, which reeks of beer and food fried in breadcrumbs, seems disproportionate compared to the ten or so bedrooms and given the location of the place on the edge of a forest. There is still this drab solemnity, this arid, lugubrious minimalism, a relic of the Communist era. The evening meal is not exactly thrilling: a plate of meat (*karbonade*) served with Brussels sprouts, one of the few vegetables I cannot stand, a hangover from my years at boarding school.

"We haven't come to Courland for its gastronomy," Joëlle says.

She could not have put it better. People's relationship with food seems purely functional here, but that may only be an impression. We are what we eat, popular wisdom decrees. Jean-Jacques Rousseau maintained that the English, with their love of very rare roast beef, could not but be a perverted and violent people. What are the Courlanders, then? To judge by the restaurants we've visited, the cuisine is peasant-based. Pork and potatoes reign supreme. Herring with onions and sour cream, and salmon with dill are both delicious, but it is rare that we are offered these. On the other hand, we never tire of the countless varieties of soft rye bread, flavoured with linseed, sesame or cumin.

All the culinary smells have congregated in our bedroom. There is not even a bedside light. The bulb in the ceiling imparts a pale yellow glow. I am tackling Keyserling's *Beate und Mareile*. I start as if I am entering a familiar house; I more or less know how things are going to turn out. This sensation of moving into known territory is most agreeable. I know nothing of the author's life. A friend advised me to read him before I left France, pointing out that Keyserling had been born in Courland and that his novels were set in the world of the Baltic barons.

On opening *Beate und Mareile*, I notice that the book contains an afterword by one of the translators, Peter Krauss. It provides precious information about the writer and his work. Born in 1855 on an estate in Courland, Keyserling spent part of his youth travelling in Germany and Italy before settling permanently in Munich in 1900. He was very ugly and at the age of forty-five already looked like an old man. Having become blind in 1907, he died in 1918. A fairly ordinary existence, were it not that it concealed a mysterious and, so it appears, infamous

episode during his youth. Whatever this was – a debt of honour, probably – obliged Keyserling to interrupt his studies at the University of
Dorpat, in Estonia, and return to Courland. At the behest of his family,
whose numerous estates he would go on to manage, he had to be satisfied with the job of steward. It was not until 1986 that his works were
translated into French.* Peter Krauss emphasizes quite correctly that
the plots of Keyserling's novels are always the same, with the same
character types: an apparently happy couple who in fact are dissatisfied, an intruder (a man or woman) who exposes the tension, children
and one or two elderly characters, not forgetting the tutor or governess
and the servants.

"This universe can easily be parodied", Krauss remarks. But Keyserling created a world that was very much his own, and one that is easily
recognizable. Rather like Simenon, in whose books the rain, for example, never falls as it does in other writers' books. Keyserling's favourite
season, curiously, was summer, a transient period in the Baltic countries. The majority of his novels unfold in an atmosphere of summer
heat and warm emotions. He had a very personal sense of light which,
in these latitudes, has an indefinable brightness and clarity, as if it were
the dawn of the world.

The paradox is that this unattractive man, for whom women would
always be unapproachable and who only associated with prostitutes,
described the fickleness and light-headedness of love wonderfully well.
Everything in his work that brings to life a person in love is there before
our eyes. His characters always behave in the same way as they head
towards disaster. From the first pages, we know his method, and we
think we are immune, yet his spellbinding power grabs us every time.

In the middle of the night, I am awakened by noises coming from
the corridor.

III

THE PROFESSOR

IN THE CORRIDOR

The noise began with muffled footsteps; I was vaguely conscious of them as I slept. The murmur escalated into a commotion that eventually resonated throughout the hotel. Falling asleep, I had been aware of loud voices in the adjoining room, as well as a rasping fit of coughing that was painful to listen to. Finding it impossible to get back to sleep, I decided to get dressed and find out what was going on.

At the reception desk I recognize the German couple we had noticed at Laidi during the day. The woman is distraught in her blue silk dressing-gown. Her feet are bare. The husband, who has dressed hurriedly in a T-shirt and Bermuda shorts, is trying to comfort her. He lays his hands gently on her shoulders. She pulls away almost violently.

The hotel's manager, who speaks neither German nor English, realizes that he needs to call a doctor. He waves the telephone around in a helpless sort of way. Apparently, there is no answer. The woman insists angrily. Her fierce and haggard expression is deeply moving; without make-up, her naked, animated, unrestrained face is very beautiful. She exchanges brief words with her husband, her voice like a hiss. I rush to our bedroom to wake Joëlle.

"You must come at once; you are needed."

I have forgotten to mention that my wife is a doctor. Within a few seconds she is dressed and rushing off to the reception desk. She introduces herself in English.

"We speak French," the man cuts in. "Hurry, please."

I dislike his peremptory tone, but there are extenuating circumstances. Letting Joëlle go to what turns out to be his sick daughter's room, I reimmerse myself in Keyserling.

Hard to concentrate. Joëlle returns a few minutes later for her doctor's bag. The situation appears to be serious. Fairly quickly, however, I have the impression that on the other side of the wall the voices are calming down and being replaced by whispering.

"More fear than harm. Bronchitis brought on by asthma. It's always dramatic; you think they're suffocating. By chance, I had a Ventolin inhaler in my bag. The effect is striking; the bronchitis stops straight away. A real magic wand! She's asleep now. The parents kissed my hands. To listen to them, you would think I'd saved their daughter's life. They shouldn't get so carried away. In fact, they rather annoyed me: they wanted to pay me! In any case, they've invited us to the restaurant. I don't think we can get out of it."

They live in Westphalia, but the man's family is from Königsberg, in east Prussia, now known as Kaliningrad. He teaches in a school of industrial design. A *Herr Doktor*. He speaks French quite well, with the characteristic German intonation, formal and leaden, and a mangling of consonants. I'm unable to discover the reasons for his journey to Courland. He seems very well informed about its history, in any case.

"You may remember we bumped into each other at Laidi."

"It's possible. I'm so absent-minded. What did you think of it?"

"So far I've only seen two palaces: Laidi and Kazdanga."

"The Germans are unaware of the extraordinary fate of these *Baltenritter*, the descendants of the Teutonic Knights. It was their own fault that they were expelled from an earthly paradise. They didn't see the danger coming, even though the portents were piling before their eyes. Their attitude was suicidal: they lived in a timeless world, with their horses, their peasants, their servants. They didn't know how to husband their good fortune."

Is this not the story of *The Leopard*? It is all the more astonishing since the author of that novel, Giuseppe di Lampedusa, knew the world of the Baltic barons between the wars. During the 1930s, he spent his summer holidays at the manor house of Stomersee (nowadays Stamerienas, in the province of Vidzeme). The family of his wife, Alexandra von Wolff, known as Licy, who were descended from the Teutonic Knights, had succeeded in preserving this estate after nationalization in 1920 – the Wolffs were among the largest Baltic landowners, with 290,000 hectares and some thirty country houses. The Professor has never read *The Leopard*, but he thinks he has seen the film. I ask whether he knows Keyserling's books. I am disappointed; he has never heard of them, but he does know of another Keyserling, Hermann, a German thinker of the inter-war years and a committed European – none other than the writer's nephew. Perhaps the Professor is not interested in literature. I talk about Ernst Jünger. He laughs in my face in such an impudent way that I suddenly feel almost offended.

"I don't understand the fascination of the French for this writer. It is true that he did everything to present himself to them in the best light. You see him as an anti-Nazi, forgetting the extreme opinions he held during the 1920s. He played a part in the rise of Hitler."

Even though I retort that Jünger made up for this by writing *On Marble Cliffs*, an anti-Hitler book, the Professor doesn't want to know about it.

"One can't spend one's entire life being responsible for one's mistakes. Don't you believe in redemption?"

He is silent. I discover that he teaches budding designers, practical men, creators of new forms. He regards me somewhat severely.

"A designer is not someone who forgets the past. Although he has to be aware of his own times, he must also rely on culture, on artistic knowledge, on experience. Designing decorative objects without doing any research is uninteresting. Form must follow function."

I don't know any designers personally, but I am conscious, like everyone else, of industrial design and the shape of everyday objects such as cars, computers, stereos, furniture.

This morning, while we are having breakfast, a beautiful June light, straight out of Keyserling, sweeps through the huge dining hall. A clarity in the air that is quite unlike anything in our own countries. The sun has risen over the forest with wonderfully accurate slowness and lightness. The daylight had not disappeared completely. That is the miracle of these northern lands where dusk and dawn merge. I have noticed that the houses have no shutters. Worn out, no doubt, by the long winter nights, people want to savour the fullness of the endless summer days.

The air has an incredible shimmering quality. It even manages to transfigure our hotel, which gleams. The dark mass of the neighbouring forest sets off the front of the building and the terrace. The Professor is gulping down litres of tea and sampling salmon and sausages with an enjoyment that is delightful to witness.

"It was fortunate that you thought to come out of your room; it was you who raised the alarm. Ach! I hate to imagine what might have happened . . . May I suggest the following: we shall organize a picnic. I'll take care of everything. What about the grounds of a country estate? Do you have a preference?"

"We had planned to visit Pelci. It's not far from here; what do you reckon?"

His affable expression changes all of a sudden. He gives me a curious look.

"Pelci! The Germans call it Pelzen. I suppose you know its history?"

"Not especially. I know it's a rather interesting Art Nouveau structure. I believe I'm right in thinking it was built around 1900."

"That's correct. It's the work of the great architect Wilhelm von Neumann. But the house is more in the Neo-Renaissance style. It's the decorations that are Art Nouveau."

It is obvious that the Professor is not telling me everything. However, he does explain that this is his second trip to Courland; he came last year with his wife. The son, who is hyperactive and somewhat detatched, is playing ball in the hotel garden. The convalescent daughter is a fairly plump, blonde little girl. The mother, with her nonchalant yet assiduous manner, exudes a sweetness still tinged with anxiety. She gazes fondly at her daughter. The father lays his maps out in front of me, occasionally raising his head and looking at me rather vaguely.

"Does the car belong to you?" he says, pointing at the Skoda.

I reply that I've rented it.

"It's different from the other Eastern makes. The Favorit's design was modified in the workshop of the great Italian coachbuilder Bertone."

We arrange to meet in the grounds of Pelci at 1.00 p.m. I insist on bringing the wine.

The grounds are vast and extend right up to the house, a red-brick building in very good condition. The Professor's family are waiting for us beneath an oak tree, with an incredible array of food laid out on a white tablecloth: ham, sausages, herring, salmon, smoked eel, rows of cold meat, blinis and *piroshki*s, together with masses of receptacles: small bowls, cups, ramekins, dishes containing sauces and condiments, fromage frais, clotted cream, gherkins, onions, beetroot and cabbage salads.

How have they procured all this food? I have visited a few shops; the choice is generally pretty basic. I had the greatest difficulty finding two bottles of wine: a Georgian white and a Crimean red from Yalta.

I am beginning to feel anxious about how we will ever cope with such abundance, but am soon tucking in. All the dishes and condiments are delicious. Alas, my Georgian wine smells of nail varnish. As for the Crimean red, it is acidic and characterless. The Professor smacks his lips with satisfaction. I am very careful not to disrupt his pleasure. Having undone the laces of his suede tennis shoes in the way that other people loosen their ties, he raises a solemn toast to Joëlle, "the distinguished doctor whom Providence placed in our path."

There is no doubting the kindliness of these Germans: they are bending over backwards to be pleasant to us, but this over-effusive cordiality eventually creates if not embarrassment, then a degree of overly intimate awkwardness. Eating, for them, is an apparently serious, in any case a thoughtful, business. The Professor munches away, his expression ponderous, unsmiling. His wife Louise does her solemn best to restore order to the victuals which we have seen fit to misplace and muddle up. "Taking pot luck" is not an expression with which these two are likely to be familiar. Nobody speaks.

I don't know why such "pauses" – those moments of silence when an angel passes overhead – have always frightened me. It is my misfortune to be obsessive about filling such gaps. I constantly need to revive the conversation, and I do so with a zeal that can quickly appear suspicious and which only adds to the awkwardness. I stammer and stutter and get in a muddle. I ask questions and don't listen to the replies.

The Professor and his wife are perfectly at ease with the silence. They have nothing to say because they are eating. Satisfy one's hunger rather than one's appetite; that seems to be their attitude. The ebb and flow of conversation, which is what is supposed to make picnics so delightful, has given way to the vague sounds of a distant ball game, to the soughing of the breeze ruffling the trees in the park, to the soft tinkling of cutlery as it comes into contact with the tablecloth laid on the grass. Basically, everything is fine. It is just me imagining things again.

"Pelci . . ." The Professor wipes his mouth. He has finished and is about to speak. "Pelci, yes, what do you think of the place?"

"Pleasant. Peaceful, certainly. A slightly melancholy, even disturbing, beauty."

He invites me to tour the buildings. The strange mascarons adorning each of the many windows feature the heads of gods or Germanic warriors. No two subjects are identical.

"Have you noticed the figures? They look like something out of the *Nibelungen*. That head of a woman, it's Brunhilde. This one, with the very cruel expression, looks like Hagen. All this is very German."

He says this with obvious irony. What is he driving at?

"It's a place that can only give pleasure to Germans. The dense, dark forest, these legendary characters . . . It makes sense: the house belonged to the Lievens. In Courland, you keep coming across the same, originally German, families: the Lievens, the Osten-Sackens, the Pahlens, the Manteuffels, the Medems, all descended from the Teutonic Knights. They intermarried and built palaces for their children. Laidi, where we met, belonged to the Manteuffels, as did Kazdanga, which you have already visited."

The house is closed. We can tell by looking through the windows of the empty rooms.

"I believe it's a primary school nowadays. This is what has saved these houses. The Communist regime didn't destroy them; it converted

them into technical colleges, municipal libraries, retirement homes . . .
But Pelci, that's another matter . . ."

He is beating about the bush, clearly hesitating as to whether he
should disclose something about the place.

"I was saying that this house can only have appeal for Germans.
During the last war, Pelci was the headquarters of the Wehrmacht's
Army Group Courland. The house was so well camouflaged that the
Red Army never managed to find it. It merged into the park and the
forest, and yet there were many pathways and approaches to it. You
probably know that the 'Courland cauldron' continued to simmer
until May 1945."

"You mean the Courland Pocket?"

"Yes, but here they use the term *cauldron*, as if this region had a
predisposition for turbulence, for boiling over. In 1919, as you will be
aware, Courland was in fact a genuine cauldron. It's a strange country –
un drôle de pays, as you say in France."

He accentuates the "ô" by opening his mouth very wide. He speaks
French better than I had first thought. After some uncertainty searching for words and groping for correct pronunciation, his conversation
has suddenly become more fluid. He even displays agility in the way he
employs our language. He has a rich vocabulary. His wife is less fluent,
but she makes fewer grammatical errors.

"You mean 'odd', 'surprising'?"

"It's hard to describe. The French word expresses that indefinable,
unexpected character very well. You French say, '*C'est drôle*', which I
think also means 'comical' or 'funny'."

"We also speak of the Phoney War . . ."

There I may have gone a bit too far. It occurs to me that just when
one is feeling at ease with a German, the fatal moment arrives when

the vexed subject presents itself in a question such as: "What were you up to, you and your parents, between 1933 and 1945?" The Professor does not flinch. He regards me out of the corner of his eye with an expression I have not seen before, a mixture of humour and subterfuge.

"In Germany we call it the 'sitting war'."

He is silent for a long while. All that can be heard is the buzzing of insects, a heavy, dull hum in keeping with the abundant vegetation suddenly released from its winter inertia.

"I told you that I was born in Königsberg. I was one year old when my mother managed to escape on one of the last ships to leave east Prussia. My father was a sub-lieutenant in the Wehrmacht. He died in April 1945 on the Courland front, very near here. I am pleased that we were able to locate his grave last year. Under Communism, we had no idea where he was buried. That's how we have come to know and love this land. You discover many hidden gems, but you have to look for them. It's a real treasure hunt. Take this grand house. You've seen all that carved clover, those oak leaves and flowers? I am convinced that the architect intended all those symbols to have hidden meanings."

He points out a series of capitals depicting birds pecking at pine kernels.

"Just look at that; it's repeated all over the place. I believe it's meant to describe an execution. The fruit of the conifer devoured by birds represents the killing of the tree's spirit. It's a very ancient theme: the king is killed so that his soul can be transmitted to his successor. The architect, von Neumann, knew the work of James George Frazer; Frazer's book *The Golden Bough* was very popular in Germany. The king of the forest who is killed so that his spirit can be reborn in the person of his successor is a leitmotif that can be found in a number of stories from Saxony, Bavaria and Prussia. These stories are also

107

common in Baltic and Scandinavian countries. The decay of vegetative life in winter is interpreted as a degeneration of nature, which has become old and deciduous. It must therefore be rejuvenated in springtime by putting it to death so that it can recover its strength in a more youthful form. The pine kernel has always been a symbol of fecundity, of reproduction, of eternal renewal."

He points out the decorative patterns featuring weapons grouped around a helmet and surmounted by gryphons, eagles, lions and dragons. He pauses before a window.

"'My youth is renewed like the eagle's.' Psalm 103. Yet another symbol of resurrection!"

I am not sure whether all these trophies really have any significance, as he delights in insisting that they do. He speaks of resurrection, possibly because of his daughter being well again, whereas the place gives me the opposite sense of death, of stillness – a malign feeling. This German romanticism with its golden chalices and knights, all this symbolism of destruction and regeneration, makes me feel ill at ease.

The Professor obviously knows his subject; moreover, he has that rare quality of not trying to impose his opinions. He never stops punctuating his remarks with reservations: "it seems to me", "in my view". Beyond his love of Courland and the history of its grand houses, it is clear that he is pursuing an aim or a quest to do with the death of his father. There is something painful about his search. It is evidently an ordeal for him.

The daughter offers Joëlle the bunch of flowers she has gathered. She has picked not just wild flowers but also irises and hyacinths from the flowerbeds belonging to the house. The father scolds her gently – at least that is what I imagine from his tone and the child's slightly contrite smile.

Regarding me somewhat ironically, he wipes his gold-rimmed spectacles with the hem of his polo shirt.

"I am grateful to you, as a Frenchman, for not having asked me whether the end of the war and the fall of Hitler marked the defeat or the liberation of the Germans. It is clear that we have all been tainted. You know that passage from the Bible: 'The fathers have eaten sour grapes and the children's teeth are set on edge.' Our fathers' generation are collectively responsible for the crimes of the Nazis. Their shame is reflected on us, and it's not a ... *fertile* feeling, is that how you say it in French? Ninety per cent of Latvia's Jews were exterminated. After Estonia, that's the highest proportion in Europe. More than elsewhere, the Latvian population took part in the massacres, but that doesn't reduce our responsibility in any way. I never knew my father. He occupied this country. How did he conduct himself? Honestly, I have no idea. The letters he sent to my mother have all been lost. But I've found a few photographs that she must have treasured."

He takes one out of his wallet. It is tiny, with serrated edges. It shows a man in Wehrmacht uniform and cap; his features are difficult to make out. He is standing by some steps leading up to a brick building.

"I think that's Pelci. You can understand my confusion when you suggested we meet in the grounds of this particular house."

I look closely at the building in the photograph. It requires a great effort of the imagination to believe that it is Pelci. It is true that the staircase is similar to those at the rear of the house, but one can only make out the steps and a minute segment of brick wall. I am careful not to let the Professor see that I am sceptical. "Fascinating," I murmur hypocritically. "An extraordinary coincidence."

"Isn't it?" he replies, his expression suggesting gratitude. Suddenly, that way he has of peering at the person he is addressing while wiping his spectacles no longer seems so awkward. This quest for his father, as well as the fantasy he has created for himself, move me deeply. Having discovered his father's grave the previous year, here he is, reconstructing, in his own way, the final months of his father's life.

"I'm a true Prussian. You French, you're completely wrong about Prussia: the militarism, the rigidity, the Junkers – it's a caricature of the German character. Did you know that the Nazis had a tough time establishing themselves in Königsberg?"

"This Jünger whom you dislike wrote the following in his diary: 'The verdict brought upon the Prussians is one of the most reliable of intelligence tests.'"*

In the park, the little girl is fully absorbed in enjoying herself on a swing. Louise, her mother, is pushing her energetically. The child flies higher and higher. As we look on, the Professor says, laughing, "It'll be a good harvest." I don't pay much attention to his remark, but I feel anxious.

"Is she going to fall off?"

He shakes his head.

"It's just a game they play. Perhaps you know that Courlanders used to apply themselves diligently to this exercise, but not to amuse themselves. You had to swing as high as you possibly could to guarantee a good harvest."

There are some landscapes or houses that lie in wait. Such places rely upon an event or a person for them to reveal themselves. Pelci, clearly, is not waiting any more. It no longer has a part to play. Dedicated to the education of children, it is unlikely that its role will ever change again.

The Professor has knocked back the bottle of red wine virtually on his own. His face is flushed. I don't dare ask him whether he enjoyed this particular Crimean vintage. He sluices the liquid round his palate like a true connoisseur.

"Obviously, it's a little tart. I prefer our Rhine wines. It's a pity; I've never tasted Courland wine. Apparently it packs quite a punch."

"You're joking. Vines in this part of the world?"

"It's surprising, I grant you. There is a vineyard not far from here called Sabile. Why don't we go and have a look round to complete this pleasant day?"

THE SABILE VINEYARD

The Professor has asked me whether, as a favour, he might drive the Skoda Favorit. Our wives have set off together in the Volvo. He drives steadily, taking routes that do not feature on the map. Many of the roads in Courland are not tarmacked. They are gravel tracks which, in this very dry month of June, throw up clouds of dust which linger in the air for a long time. Fortunately, Joëlle and the Professor's wife are not following us; they have taken another route. My companion insists on showing me, not far from the vineyard, a group of manor houses that are "absolutely unique", as he puts it.

The hum of the engine, the comfort of the car and the driver's assurance put me at my ease. I talk to him about the Resurrector. I expect the Professor to be astonished, as people have been before when I have raised the subject, but he does not seem at all surprised. He knows of the man's existence. He also knows that he works for the V.D.K., the German organization with headquarters in Kassel that concerns itself with finding the burial places of Wehrmacht soldiers and, if possible, the dates of their deaths. The Professor had been in touch with the V.D.K. about his father. He did not immediately understand the term "*malgré-nous*", but he is aware of the men from Alsace and Moselle who were forcibly conscripted during the Third Reich: "In Germany, we know about *Gauleiter* Wagner, who took the decision to do this. He was a friend of Hitler's; he took part in the Munich Putsch and was arrested with him." I mention the impossible mission my Alsatian cousin entrusted me with before I left France. "It's very vague. One would need more facts in order to trace one's father."

We stop in a village to buy refreshments. We sit on a bench. Children are riding their bicycles around the square. The Professor greets them in Latvian. I didn't know he spoke it. A very old man with a mottled face standing at the door of his house exchanges a few words with the Professor, who looks astonished. The old fellow mutters rather than talks. There are long silences. We get back into the car.

"The man we just met was born in 1905, 'the year of the first revolution', as he put it. He was fourteen at the time of the rioting in 1919. His parents had taken shelter in the outbuildings of a nearby manor house. He remembers the German commandos, their long greatcoats that swept the ground. He was very frightened of them, but that was nothing compared with the Bolsheviks. For him and his parents, the soldiers of the Red Army were the Devil incarnate. What the refugees feared was a breakthrough on the front line. It's odd: he is still obsessed by this detail seventy-five years on, the long German greatcoats streaking through the snow."

At full tilt, the Skoda leaves a huge dust plume behind it. Gravel peppers the chassis. Won't the poppy-red paintwork be damaged?

"It's a tenacious car. Skoda existed long before Communism."

We pass through ghost villages with their old Germanic churches and a few wooden houses. It's astonishing to see dilapidated modern blocks in these deserted little towns. They were created under the Soviet system to keep an eye on the peasants, who had previously been scattered here and there.

Thick grass covers the fresh-looking fields. Well nourished by the abundant spring rain and the never-ending June light, nature displays an almost tropical lushness. There is an explosive quality about the vegetation in this land, shackled for so long by winter. It is like a dam that has just burst, dispersing inexhaustible, lustrous flora over the Courland countryside.

The car comes to a sudden stop beneath a vast oak tree. The Professor asks me to turn round. I see a group of magnificent, ruined manor houses which together form a sort of quadrilateral. The main house is a white eighteenth-century building in the Rococo style. The front steps are worn away. Today the ground floor serves as the municipal library and information centre.

"Fortunately the house still has a use; otherwise it would no longer be here. I wanted to show you Kabile. Legend has it that the Romanov dynasty came from this village. In any case, Kabile gives an idea of that vanished world I have mentioned. Nothing else is left of those Baltic barons. As I told you: they saw nothing coming, just like your French nobility in 1789!"

In the grounds is an old man with a rake. The Professor calls out to him. Where did he learn Latvian? A conversation begins. The man has the tired yet alert face of those who have been through hard times but who have not lost their enthusiasm for life.

"He says that the few foreigners he has encountered are only interested in the manor houses and the history of the Baltic barons. He thinks that because I am German, I can only be a descendant of one of those families who keep returning to this country. However much I deny it, he doesn't believe me. He also claims that you are the first Frenchman he's ever set eyes on. He is very impressed."

"Ask him what he's doing here."

The old man chuckles, shrugs and sets off on a long explanation which the Professor, turning back to me, eventually interrupts.

"He was a teacher, apparently, but his pension is very small. He has been taken on by the village as a caretaker. 'I try to push back nature's excesses': that's how he put it, but he is grateful to have been entrusted with the task. He feels happy in this park, surrounded by these ruined buildings. It's his kingdom. In his opinion, none of this disrepair should be interfered with since it has attained a perfect balance. Between ourselves, I get the feeling that he dreads seeing the house restored one day."

"And what will he do when the roofs collapse? The balance will be wrecked . . ."

The Professor translates while the old man looks up at the sky and points. This time he uses fewer words.

"He says, 'The Courlanders are in a hole. They like it there and don't want to climb out of it.'" The Professor turns back to me. "But we ought to go. Our wives are waiting."

The old gardener waves goodbye, one hand resting on his rake. Around his waist, a red cord, the kind used to tie back curtains, holds up his worn trousers.

"We have found a Courland Diogenes: 'Keep away from my ruins!'" The Professor laughs at his little joke. "He was suspicious to begin with. After independence, businessmen appeared on the scene, foreigners visiting these manor houses with the idea of converting them into luxury hotels. I think it's still too soon for that, but it's unavoidable, alas. There's nothing the old man can do to prevent it."

The Professor looks thoughtful. I still haven't dared to ask him where he learnt Latvian. After a long silence, he relates something else the old man told him.

"Because I am German, he asked whether I was searching for graves. I didn't understand. Then he explained that in the neighbouring village a man had spent several days digging holes in the ground.

He brought along an excavator, but they didn't find anything. So he left again. I think it was your Resurrector."

I suddenly feel annoyed with the Professor: why did he not tell me this when we were with the gardener? He understands why I might feel piqued, even though the excavating episode took place over two weeks ago. And the gardener, who had not even seen the man in question, didn't know where he'd gone afterwards. My irritation subsides, but I curse the fact that I had come so close to the man who had given me the slip in Liepaja. That was also two weeks ago, I tell myself, and I don't even know the name of the village where those excavations took place. The Professor consoles me: Courland is not that big. Who knows, perhaps I'll come across the Resurrector on another occasion? Now, we're off to Sabile and its vineyard, where Joëlle, Louise and the two children are waiting.

Empty hamlets, abandoned smallholdings, alternating meadows and forests, plenty of orchards. Piles of timber lying beside footpaths and in clearings and stumps left in the ground continually remind one of Courland's wooded landscape. The sand sticking to the roots of these vegetal accumulations brings them eerily to life. They look like cavities in a monstrous jaw. The pagan memory of this land allows powerful forces to lie dormant within it. The omnipresent forest is a living being.

The Professor questions me about the *malgré-nous* who fought in Courland. I did a little research into the matter before my departure. A hundred and thirty thousand men from Alsace and Moselle had been dragooned into the Wehrmacht. It would appear that Hitler had not been keen initially about incorporating them into the German army; he did not consider them to be reliable. But in 1942 *Gauleiter* Wagner persuaded him to do it. According to Wagner, this was a good way of making them proper citizens of the Reich. The majority of these soldiers, sent to distant front lines such as Russia, were spread among different units to avoid any connivance between them.

As to how many Alsatian men died on the battlefields of Courland, I reply that it is impossible to obtain a precise figure. The total number of men from Alsace and Moselle killed in battle during the Second World War is 40,000, not counting the 12,000 who disappeared or never returned from the Soviet camps. The Professor insists on having a rough idea of the amount. I give in, and reply that it was about a hundred, well aware that I have no grounds for saying this.

We suddenly arrive in the village of Sabile, with its wooden houses, its Lutheran church and its bridge over the River Abava. The Skoda is completely covered in dust.

It seems incredible that a vineyard should be hidden away in a place like this! On closer inspection, however, I realize that the area is surrounded by hills. The Abava valley is a curiosity known as "Courland's Switzerland". It would be wrong to exaggerate: it is composed not of mountains but of a series of rounded hills. The ruins of a medieval castle stand atop one of them. Joëlle beckons to us and points out a fairly steep hill: the Sabile vineyard. She and the Professor's wife are talking to a man aged about twenty who speaks English quite well. He explains that vines have been grown in Sabile since the reign of Jacob Kettler, the seventeenth-century Duke of Courland. "You can always make a vine grow, but does it produce grapes?" Louise says. I reply that the grapevine is a plant that can adapt anywhere and that it thrives at pretty much any latitude: "They even make wine in Quebec, even though the winters are long and hard, and spring comes late." I have read in Roger Dion's book* that in the thirteenth century the Teutonic Knights succeeded in making vines grow on the sandy hills of Thorn, in east Prussia.

"How do you know that?"

"Wine is my hobby."

"But wine is a pleasure, not a pastime!"

The young man is proud to show off the "wine hill", as he calls it. He is wearing new trainers with non-skid soles. While admiring his state-of-the-art buskins, he explains that in the nineteenth century the vineyard fell into disuse, but that it was revived in 1936 at the initiative of President Karlis Ulmanis. Karlis Ulmanis is a name I have heard on several occasions during this trip. From a Courland peasant family, he studied agriculture in the United States, graduating from the University of Nebraska. It was of the utmost importance to him to revive this historic vineyard. Unfortunately, the war came, and the "wine hill" was neglected. Later, an experimental team wanted to replenish the vineyard, but the people in charge moved on, and the quality of work declined. It was not until 1989 that a group of students set about restoring the hillside. It was the first president of the new Republic of Latvia, Guntis Ulmanis, the great-nephew of the former president, who inaugurated its revival by planting an apple tree at the vineyard's foot.

A crowd has gathered around us. They show us over the vineyard. Large quantities of vines have been planted on the narrow hillside. We press the young English speaker for details. We're under the impression that the Sabile vineyard only produces white wine. Is it any good? "Excellent," a pink-cheeked man assures us. This remark, translated by our young interpreter, evokes scepticism among the villagers. "It's a curiosity. To say that the wine is good . . ."

There are apricot, peach and nut trees at the top of the hill. The chatter and laughter of the people gathered at the foot of the vineyard lend a cheerful atmosphere to this impromptu gathering. The Professor, who has not said a word, starts to speak. The ten or so people making up the little group are struck dumb, but it is definitely the young interpreter who is the most astonished. He looks amazed. A foreigner who speaks Latvian! (In this country of 2.3 million inhabitants, it is important to remember that Latvian is the mother tongue of only 1.3 million of them, and that it was in danger of disappearing altogether during the Soviet occupation.)

What can the Professor have to say to our little group? When his speech comes to an end, a long silence ensues, a silence so impressive that I have the feeling that his listeners have not understood a word. In fact, they are flabbergasted. They all begin chattering at once. I imagine they are saying, "Who is this guy?" "Where did he learn our language?" "Unbelievable!"

What a commotion! The Professor feigns a troubled expression. I have noticed that he sometimes puts on the theatrical air that good teachers adopt to keep their students on tenterhooks. He has a way of gauging the effect of what he is saying down to the last detail: "I asked them whether we could taste the wine. It's a bit complicated. One can't drink it until the Wine Festival, in July. The cellar is closed. In any case, production is very small. They say that the surface area of the vineyard is about 1.5 hectares, but that sounds a bit much to me." He is amazed by all the fuss. Latvians, more especially Courlanders, generally keep their distance. They don't talk easily to foreigners. They regard shyness as a virtue.

While the people continue talking excitedly among themselves, I remark to the Professor that this lack of restraint is normal. The vineyard exerts a magic spell over the landscape and the people, all the more so in a land with borders such as Courland. The Professor agrees, not without irony: "'Magic spell'! That's very French: so impressive yet so vague . . ."

119

When foreigners say, "That's very French", the comment is rarely intended to be complimentary, but I take it as praise. It is true that we trot out big words; we like them to ring out, and they are often meaningless. But the day that we stop using fine words will be the ruin of us. We transform the world through our enthusiastic delusions, the only means left to charm this accountable, marketable universe.

Amid all the hubbub, one bit of information keeps being mentioned: Sabile features in the *Guinness Book of Records* as the northernmost vineyard in the world.

"They are very proud of the fact. I get the feeling that they're more interested in this achievement than in the wine."

The Professor and I decide to climb the hill. The young man with the new trainers comes with us, as does the baby-faced fellow. It's a tough climb. The young man, who does not want to dirty his beautiful clean shoes, is more troubled by this than we are; he tries to avoid the slippery patches of clay. I marvel at the view over the village and the metallic ribbon of the river. It is an unusual landscape for Courland, which most often presents an impression of flatness that can come to seem monotonous. The soil gives off a marshy smell which contrasts with the scents carried up on the breeze from the valley: the balsamic scent of juniper, the smell of distant haymaking, the green scent of leaves.

They wave at us from down below; we pay them scant attention. The view from up here changes everything. The baby-faced man is leaning against one of the peach trees that line the hillside. Closing his eyes, he breathes in deeply. The young man is gazing down at his smudged shoes; although there is mud clinging to them, he seems happy to be with us, at the summit, overlooking the vineyard. The Professor mumbles a few words in German. He is considerate enough to translate them for me afterwards: "May reason be present wherever living creatures are glad to be alive. Then the past remains constant, the future still ahead comes to life, the moment is eternity . . ." Apparently from a well-known poem by Goethe, "Vermächtnis".* "Yes, only the present moment counts, it is really the only thing that depends on us."

I jot down these lines in my notebook. The four of us look at one another knowingly. What have we done? Viewed from close to, the hill is quite small; the vineyard does exist, but it is tiny. As for the climb, only the start was difficult, and we are hardly on the roof of the world. Nevertheless, the young man points out that the hill is thirty-three metres high!

So why should we have the sense that we have experienced a moment of fulfilment? Only four of us chose to attempt the ascent. We believe that we have been favoured. The effort has made us feel lighter. Up here, we feel as though a weight has lifted, as if we left the earth at the foot of the hill.

A stork appears overhead, its neck extended. I contemplate its soaring flight with a touch of jealousy. I ask myself whether I need to go any higher. The Professor waits for the bird to be right above his head before hailing it joyfully with a wave of his hand. The voice of wisdom: he looks neither forwards nor back. The Professor is clearly concentrating on the present.

On this late afternoon, the sun is still high in the sky, the air sparkles, noises both gentle and shrill rise from the village, rather like the sounds of percussion instruments: a hammer being struck, the fleeting noise of car horns, the soft put-putting of a tractor engine, the sound of a saw on wood. They resonate through me like an illumination. I feel in communion with the world. In that instant I may have had my first true vision of Courland, my perfect moment, a familiar image without manor houses, without history, without golden boughs. It could have been anywhere in Europe.

We walk down the hill in silence. This being June, the vines have not yet grown very much, but they will catch up in a few weeks' time. It is not so much the lack of warmth as the absence of light that prevents the grapes from ripening. This is where this vineyard has the advantage. Throughout the long days of June and July, the clear light remains constant, encouraging photosynthesis.

Joëlle and the Professor's wife ironically applaud our arrival at the bottom of the hill: "Bravo. What an expedition!" We are expected in the cellar, which has been opened specially, for a tasting. Candles stuffed into the necks of flasks, bottles placed neatly on shelves, ancient phials of blown glass: most of the characteristics of a wine cellar are here. It smells like an old, disused kitchen dresser. The cellar-man pulls gently on a cork, taking care to smell it in the way that ignorant sommeliers do who want to impress their customers. It is a perfectly pointless exercise: a cork will always smell of cork, and it is impossible, at this stage, to discover whether it has affected the taste of the wine.

The Professor has pointed out that I am French. With amusement bordering on mockery, everyone looks at me swirling my glass before smelling the wine. The colour is pale, but that does not mean anything. In the mouth, the wine is bitter, rough, even harsh; it certainly lacks subtlety, yet I am agreeably surprised. "It has a kick," I tell the Professor. He translates, but at great length. I suspect him of embellishing. "I said that you were very impressed by the quality of the wine and its flowery nose. 'Flowery' is kind, and they are pleased. Personally, I find the wine rather feudal in its roughness, but, to tell the truth, I don't know much about wine." *Feudal* ... where did he find this actually rather appropriate word? The wine is in fact compelling in its harshness.

The pink-cheeked man, who is sampling the wine with us, knocks his glass back in one gulp. He keeps on asking for more, declaring as he does so, "It's good. I am drinking of freedom." "Doesn't he mean that he is drinking *to* freedom?" No, no, he is drinking *of* freedom, "for," he says, "the Sabile vines have only really produced when the country was free and independent." He asserts that under totalitarian regimes it is impossible to make wine worthy of the name. He compares Communism to an axe; in his opinion, one cannot cultivate vines with an axe. He drinks a toast to "beautiful freedom".

These libations are set to last, but the Professor's little girl is showing signs of weariness and tugging at her mother's sleeve. Unconcerned by the excitement, her brother is bouncing his ball against the cellar wall. Sadly, we must be on our way. I was just beginning to get used to Sabile, to the wine-producing hill situated on the 57th parallel, to the cordiality of these Courlanders we met at the vineyard's foot.

The last image I take away with me is of the young man's trainers. Their soles, which resemble the tyres on a mountain bike, are so encrusted that he has difficulty lifting his feet. He doesn't care. He seems liberated. "He didn't think twice about getting them dirty," Louise says in the car. "You put him through a real initiation."

We salute his courage by waving wholeheartedly through the window.

FLUFFY SOVIET BLANKETS

"So, what do you make of our new friends?"

"Instead of a Latvian, we have a Prussian showing us around Courland! He seems extremely well informed."

"Your independence matters so much to you . . . you're going to have him on your back for the rest of the trip . . ."

"I wouldn't mind in the least. But he and his family may have other plans. We shall see at the hotel this evening. And his wife, what do you think of her?"

"Louise? She's nice, but she's a bit annoyed with her husband. She would have preferred to go to Sicily."

"Does she loathe Courland?"

"Not at all. She, like us, is fascinated by this different yet familiar country. She confessed that her husband's stories about Baltic barons bore her stiff. That's not the case with me, as you might imagine. Obviously, I'm more interested in the present moment, but I understand why you find these speculations about the past so fascinating."

A message from Henri is waiting for me at the hotel; I had managed to forget all about him. I'm an ungrateful beast despite the fact that I owe my discovery of this region to him. However much I rack my memory, this trip is unlike any of the others I have taken. Nothing happens as one might expect it to. All these chance encounters evoke a reality that I am unable to define. And these characters, how am I going to use them in my article? To what extent will this report I

124

am assembling for Henri be "real"? Ever since I've been a journalist, I've never stopped asking myself how it is that the truth should be so untruthful. It is as if the lecturer from Liepaja, the Karosta rocker and the Professor had spread the word. Having encountered a man pursuing a fantasy, they said to themselves, "Courland is so unreal. We ourselves don't know exactly what it is. He has taken the trouble to come this far; let's not disappoint him. Let's help him, let's give him what he desires!"

Henri is becoming more and more stressed. I no longer recognize the subtle, nonchalant saviour of a troubled magazine, confident in his assessments and actions. He pours out his feelings, employing his mechanic's vocabulary as usual. He talks of compression, output, friction, poor transmission. I cannot see what he is driving at. Perhaps he needs someone to talk to? He scarcely asks about Courland; it seems the least of his worries: "So, how's it going with the manor houses? Lucky devil, I'd love to be in your shoes . . ." How many times have I heard the boss come out with this remark, intended for the ears of cub reporters! Naturally, they don't pay a blind bit of attention. Only power interests them: they listen, they sympathize, they agree as a way of maintaining control. Journalists are by their very nature dissatisfied; they need to be flattered. The sharpest among them know that in fact they control nothing. They are merely watchdogs. Their position confers authority but not power. I thought Henri had no illusions about this. His anxiety makes me think otherwise. I ring off using the same old words: "I'm really getting a feel for the place now, Henri."

The truth is that I don't feel anything, or rather, I "feel" too much. Too many impressions, too many trails, too little that is concrete. Nevertheless, I am beginning to have a notion of what I shall say: Courland is not sure of its own existence. The calamitous Soviet occupiers,

125

who crushed and shattered its individuality and its remoteness, virtually left it for dead. For the time being, vaguely aware of its curious past, it is content to stay alive via the entity that is Latvia. I shall try to show that Courland is not lacking in attributes with which to reinvent itself. I am convinced that the place will discover a new identity through the vestiges of its past. I hope that Henri will not find this approach too abstract, too "conceptual", as he would put it. I still have a few days in which to delve more deeply and provide more substance for my hypothesis.

The hotel sleeps. I am sitting with the Professor at a table on the terrace. It is 11.00 p.m. and the daylight is still refusing to fade. A white, faintly ash-coloured, chalky light hangs over the countryside. In the parking lot, the Skoda, which has recovered its fine glossy red colour, seems to be aglow.

We chat as we sample an old brandy I've had in my luggage. I'd been waiting for a suitable occasion to open it. I am not sure whether the Professor is a connoisseur – he liked the second-rate wines I brought for the picnic – but he seems flattered to have qualified as a "suitable occasion". The brandy, from the Grande Champagne, is made by one of the best-known firms in Jarnac. The Professor, who has read Jean Monnet's *Mémoires*, is questioning me about the Cognac origins of this "father of Europe", but in fact he knows more than I do about Monnet's early years. As a representative of Cognac, Monnet, the founder, and first president, of the European Coal and Steel Community, was sent to Canada at the age of eighteen to visit his firm's customers.

As often happens in a conversation, one word is enough to alter the flow. Why should I have felt the need to tell the Professor that I had lived in Canada? I briefly describe my stay in Quebec, taking care not to allude to Mara. "Well, Courland should not be too unfamiliar then. The long winters, the very short days, the snow, the explosion of vegetation in spring: you would have known all that in Canada." I reply that, apart from the climate and the planning required to deal with the climate, the two countries have nothing in common. It is true that I have not experienced the Baltic winter. "The truth of this country is its winter." What truth is he talking about? "And, since we are discussing truth, I don't really understand why you chose Courland. Did you just shut your eyes and point at a map of Europe?"

The Professor does not believe in coincidences. Does he suspect that I am concealing something? He is too well brought up to question me closely. In any case, why should it matter? I realize that from the moment I first set foot in this country I have not given much thought to my Courland-Canadian lover; it's as if this land did not quite correspond to my memory of her. But in what way could this country that I am in the process of discovering equate to Mara? Among its young women I sometimes spot her type of beauty: tall, inscrutable, blonde. A vague approximation, but it suits this indeterminate place very well. I also realize that the Professor has unwittingly been captivated by Mara, as if by a twinge of remorse or recollection which I can no longer be sure is based on reality or imagination. Anyway, why should one disassociate the two? As Bachelard* said, 'To imagine is to increase the reality of a shade of colour.'

As the Professor wipes his spectacles and regards me sternly, I reflect that I don't know where Mara's family came from. She must have told me thirty years ago. Now that I am in her homeland and starting to get my bearings, I feel slightly frustrated not to remember.

As the Professor and I converse, we gaze out over the grey line of the marshes and their yellow-leaved reeds. The Courland landscape

127

would be rather dull were it not for this torpor of another age.

"It's rather like a forgotten continent. In French you use the expression 'to be inside a bubble'. Have you taken in these lanes, these villages? The countryside has not stirred for 200 years. But it's obvious that such languor cannot last. You have only to look at the furniture in this hotel. The fluffy blankets are from the Soviet era, but the bedside lights are modern – well, what they think of here as modern. It's difficult to discern, but the country is changing. Courland is used to secrecy. When you have been out of bounds for such a long time, you need to keep your hand hidden. These people are much stronger than we are, much better equipped. We've lost our instinct for survival; they've known the worst. They have had to choose and compromise. They have resisted by relying entirely on themselves. What's more, the situation continues. Since Communism collapsed, they have understood that only they can dig themselves out of the hole they're in."

"Rather like Baron Münchhausen, who was stuck in a bog, and who managed to drag himself out by his own hair."

"An amusing thought. At one point Baron Münchhausen was a candidate to rule the Duchy of Courland. He's very popular in Germany. He was a real person; he fought the Turks and then, in old age, concocted some unbelievable exploits for himself. A real mythomaniac! The story about him being chosen to rule Courland derives, apparently, from an episode in the life of Maurice de Saxe."

"The victor of Fontenoy?"

"Yes. There was some confusion between Maurice de Saxe and Münchhausen. Maurice de Saxe was elected Duke of Courland, but well before the Battle of Fontenoy, in 1725. He reigned only for two years; the Russians forced him to leave. With 500 men, he attempted to confront the army of the tsar. He took refuge very near here, on an island in Lake Usma. We could visit it tomorrow, if you like."

"I'd love to. But we have a good many places to visit and were planning to go to Ventspils."

"No problem; it's on the way. Our holiday is meant to end at Ventspils; we're catching the ferry from there to Germany the day after tomorrow."

It is midnight. The long dusk casts a grey light over the countryside, lending the sky a stormy aspect. These white nights induce an excitement bordering on euphoria, but, after a time, the confusion between light and darkness can be destabilizing. It is transformed into a feeling of frustration, as if one's being were dispossessed of its own substance. The "dark brightness" creates a ripple in the soul. I ask the Professor what he thinks of these summer nights. "They set my nerves on edge. I lose my bearings. It's like perpetual jet-lag."

Nerves on edge! It strikes me that this phrase doesn't tally with his personality . . .

MORICSALA

I have noticed that the Professor displays a certain degree of impatience towards his wife. I cannot understand what they are saying to one another, of course, but I am aware of a peremptory note in his voice, for instance this morning while we were sorting out our luggage before leaving the hotel. She replies just as sharply, but without getting flustered. Their daughter looks on with hostility.

I have the impression that the Professor is taking mischievous pleasure not so much in giving me history lessons but in showing up, with faultless affability, the countless gaps in my knowledge of Courland. He is very well informed. About the Battle of Fontenoy, for example. Frenchmen of my generation are aware that this was a victory over the British, but how would a German know that? "There's nothing astonishing about it. May I remind you that the victor's name was Maurice de Saxe. Saxony is a region of Germany!" I love Joëlle's common sense. "Well, well," she says, "you've met your match: he seems a real history buff . . ."

In a landscape in which forest and water merge, Lake Usma, with its banks of reeds dotted with birch, alder and willow saplings, remains hidden from view, only to reveal itself at the last moment. It is practically impossible to make out the shape of this watery expanse dotted with islands. Powerful eddies ripple on the surface, probably caused by fish. Echoing across the lakeside habitat, the songs of thousands of birds sound clear, fluid, almost watery. Among them I think I recognize the slightly nasal chirp of a wagtail and the persistent trill of a lapwing. A strong smell of sodden leaves, of silt and mushrooms, gusts through the air.

A fisherman points towards a strip of marshland in the distance: "Moricsala." *Sala* means "island" in Latvian. This is the "Isle of Maurice" for which we have been searching. Unfortunately, the fortification where the future victor of Fontenoy barricaded himself in 1727 can no longer be visited; it is a nature reserve, one of the oldest in Europe.

Unable to set foot on Moricsala, all we can do is imagine the 5,000 Russian soldiers stationed on this shore, waiting for Maurice de Saxe to emerge from his hiding place. He was surrounded in all directions. To gain time, he asked for ten days' grace. The answer came back that he had forty-eight hours in which to surrender. Adrienne Lecouvreur's lover realized that the game was up. But it was out of the question that he should hand himself over. He managed to escape from the island and cross the Russian lines, leaving his baggage and his supporters to his enemies. They hoped to find an important document among his belongings: the deeds of his election as ruler of Courland. But he had taken it with him; he would never allow it to leave his possession. Until the day he died, the last European *condottiere* would assert his right to the duchy. On his marble tomb in Strasbourg, sculpted by Pigalle, is the phrase "*Duc de Courlande*".

The life of the audacious Maurice de Saxe is easy to confuse with the adventurous existence of Baron Münchhausen, who in his real life as a soldier was stationed at Riga in the service of Russia; the last Catholic bishop of Courland was a Münchhausen. The Professor reckons that these two characters shared a number of characteristics, among them the ability to extricate themselves from the worst situations. The baron, though, had no equal in his ability to direct conversation towards unimportant topics chosen with care to show him off to best advantage.

On the shores of Lake Usma, I succeed in scoring a point in the unspoken sparring contest I am having with the Professor. I may well have been ignorant of aspects of the future victor of Fontenoy's Courland past, but a reference to George Sand – the Professor knows of her – prompts a gruff exclamation: "What's George Sand the writer got to do with all this?"

"You're aware that Maurice de Saxe was George Sand's great-grandfather?"

I find his scepticism mortifying. I do my best to explain the connection. George Sand's grandmother, Aurore de Saxe, was Maurice's daughter. But after that? I get slightly lost.

In the car, Joëlle makes fun of our childish games: "You've got to get used to the fact that he knows his subject perfectly. You're very fortunate."

I consult my notebook, which is full of jottings. Apart from the Resurrector's address and phone number, I brought only one name with me, that of Pope, a spot not far from Ventspils. A man from Bordeaux, Hubert Auschitzky, had given me this name. His forebear Charles, who had come from a family of Lutheran pastors, had been born in this village at the end of the eighteenth century. In the early 1820s, Charles had arrived in Bordeaux, where he had founded a company, Le Phénix, which insured the owners of vineyards, and a bank, La Bordelaise, which specialized in the wine trade. Claret is supposed to have been invented by the English, but in fact it was men like Auschitzky, who came from the Baltic, who created it. Too often it is forgotten that this wine was first introduced in the Hanseatic ports. There are wine merchants in the Chartrons district of Bordeaux, as well as vineyard owners, who still bear surnames of German origin: Bethmann, Shröder, Schyler, Cruse, Kressmann, Eschenauer.

Our route to Ventspils passes through Pope. I suggest to the Professor that we stop there.

Pope is one of these deserted Courland villages where one looks in vain for the main street and any shops. The Baroque-style church is situated on a small rise that enables one to look out over the dark mass of forests and, in the distance, the chalky-white twinkling lights of the suburbs of Ventspils. A grandiose avenue of lime trees leads from the church to the gates of the manor. The trees in our temperate regions are puny compared to these huge, full-grown specimens with their heavy, shapely trunks. They soar vertiginously towards the sun like the enormous heliophilous trees of the equatorial forests.

The grounds of the manor contain colossal oaks and ancient yews clipped in the shape of pyramids. They rise flawlessly, creating such a dense shade that the building's perimeter, at this late hour of the morning, is plunged into darkness despite the bright sunshine. Only a few tiny spots of light dapple the ground. And again there is the feeling that no-one ever comes here . . .

The silence, the ruined outbuildings, the courtyards overgrown with grass give a feeling not so much of emptiness as of a show in preparation, probably because everything converges on the well-maintained manor house. We wander among the buildings, walking to and fro across the avenue of limes, gripped by the majestic beauty of the place and its peacefulness. Still not a soul. That, for me, is Courland: an empty, depopulated land. In the villages, I haven't ever seen people conversing outdoors. Perhaps it is the harshness of the winters that makes them want to hibernate, to seek the inner life.

At the far end of the path, a shape emerges that appears to be coming towards us. It is a woman of about forty, very tall, with an impassive, even inscrutable expression. She looks straight ahead, pretending not to see us. A further example of Courland aloofness: a cautious, stern demeanour, bordering on hostility. Experience has taught us that we should not trust appearances; this unyielding wariness is merely a mask. She would never make the first approach, but if we did, everything would be possible. It is sufficient for the Professor to ask the woman a question in Latvian for her to stop and eye him suspiciously, an incredulous look on her face. She stares at each of the adults in turn. Then, when she sees the children, her expression changes. "She is the headmistress of the local school, which is located in the house. She is suggesting that we have a quick look round, as she has to get to a meeting."

Inside there is a smell of cleaning materials and cooking, as in all the schools around here. Ever since the sixteenth century, this estate of over 50,000 hectares had belonged to the von Behr family. Like the majority of the Baltic aristocracy, the owners had to leave Pope after the agrarian reforms of 1920; however, the law allowed them to retain the fifty hectares of land around the house. Apparently, one of the last barons, Karl von Behr, left (unpublished) memoirs describing the life of his social class during the late nineteenth century and up until the turmoil of 1914. The headmistress has read lengthy extracts. She speaks of them dispassionately, without resentment, like an ethnographer describing an ancient society.

Bunch of keys in hand, she opens doors mechanically, informing us that the von Behrs entertained a great deal. Visitors might stay for weeks, even months. Life was punctuated by hunts, horse racing, balls, conversation and gambling. Each year, on 10 September, the family and its servants would move to another stately home until the following 10 April. The headmistress informs us that Bismarck stayed at Pope in 1857 and shot two moose.

I remember that Hubert Auschitzky had mentioned this Karl von Behr, who had travelled all over Europe. The headmistress describes the impact of the 1905 Revolution on him and his peers. The peasantry of Pope rose up and started to burn the estate's outhouses, but the soldiers of the tsar, despatched post-haste, prevented the destruction of the manor. I have a sense of having heard it all before.

Maybe that is the missing piece! This feeling of déjà vu, the sense that the same story has been told before. The disturbing familiarity, the space in between. An absence rather than an emptiness. Comparable, not similar. The sense, too, that this country will not yield up its secrets, not because it does not have any, but because it has lost its original significance, its initial purpose. Courland, like this parkland, is deconsecrated.

I recognize the story that the headmistress is telling. The world she is describing is Keyserling's. Although she has never heard of the writer, his surname is not unfamiliar. She tells us that Baron Peter von Keyserling, an extremely colourful character, was the von Behrs' permanent guest. Was he a member of Eduard's family? She shuts the doors very carefully, sorry perhaps that the place does not retain more traces of the pomp of yesteryear. Abruptly, the Professor declares in triumphant tones, "She knows Auschitzky! He came here a few years ago. It's incredible! There's even a room that bears his name!"

The headmistress shows us into a bright room with Formica tables. Smells of damp chalk and lavender-fragranced washing-up liquid mingle with the inevitable stench of cabbage. The ceiling-mounted neon lighting is the indestructible legacy of the Soviet era. Such tubes, with their white or yellow light, attached to the ceilings of every school and public building, are distinctive in that they function only part of the time. Amid this abundance of fluorescent fixtures, there are always some that are not working or are on the blink, the characteristic of neon being either total failure or constant flickering.

The battery of neon tubes illuminating the Auschitzky Room emits light in flashes. The school furniture, however, is modern. When there are no longer any neon lights in the former Communist countries, the ghosts of dialectical materialism will have vanished for good. Fashions are already changing. A certain rusticity persists: badly cut Bolshevik blouses, dresses with excessively psychedelic patterns, heavy boots. Yet discreet make-up, elegant jewellery and silk scarves suggest a process of evolution. Always this in-between sense, this sense of time held in abeyance, this indefinable quality. Something that is vaguely similar, and then this thing that is profoundly *other*. What a mistake to think of the Baltic countries as being underdeveloped! They were not always behind. Between the two world wars, Latvia possessed an educational system and standard of living comparable to those of Western Europe. There is a vague anxiety that she may never rediscover her golden age, a fear that she will find herself stuck in a lull, in endless transition.

Our visit is over. Before taking her leave, the headmistress makes the following statement, which the Professor translates: "We are not afraid of the future. We narrowly avoided disaster. How much longer could we have carried on? Our oppressors were on the point of winning. Soon, it will be your turn. You will experience hardship, but in a different way. Of course I do not wish it upon you. We, oppressed for so long, harbour no illusions. Nothing ever truly benefits the people, but you are far less able to cope than we are."

Why this sudden prophetic tone? I sense some anxiety on the part of our guide. Her speech recalls certain remarks the Professor has made. Just the other evening, he was comparing our weakness with the strength the Latvians had derived from being enslaved for so long. He winks at me: he is drinking sour milk. The headmistress smiles: "It's always like this: the real conversations always take place as one is saying goodbye. You other Europeans, you have let us down, but we don't bear grudges. Believe it or not, Latvia has only one desire: to join the European Union."

GAMBIA AND TOBAGO

Ventspils, the former Windau, the great port of the dukes of Courland, from which, in the seventeenth century, ships set sail for the island of Tobago and for Gambia.

We have discovered a hotel on the outskirts, in the midst of prefabs built during the Khrushchev era. This newly furnished establishment is comfortable. In Courland, more than elsewhere, the choice of bedroom is a matter of luck. One rarely picks the right card, but one is never really annoyed to have lost out. An entertaining balance of power is created between each new occupant and the room's furnishings: the bulb from the overly bright bedside lamp which may have to be swapped with the one in the bathroom; the hookless hangers that collapse the moment you put the lightest item of clothing on them; the duvet, too hot for summer, that you have to remove from its cover; the missing soap; the toilet that flushes itself all night. Not to mention the ghastly prints depicting forest landscapes that need to be turned to the wall. A stealthy hand-to-hand struggle takes place. A Courland object possesses unusually powerful inertia. You must employ cunning to deal with the absolutism it attempts to impose, to circumvent rather than confront it.

This time, there's a surprise: the bed, the lighting, the sanitary fittings are all agreeable. Everything is new. This is not luxury, but the modernity is conciliatory and does not balk in the face of new arrivals. The television works; we can even get French T.V.5.

The Professor and his wife have gone to the port to make enquiries about their departure. I plan to visit the castle situated at the mouth of the Venta, whence the name Ventspils, "castle on the Venta". A tourist leaflet in English intended for the hotel's guests explains that the fortress was built at the end of the thirteenth century by the Livonian Knights.

With their extraordinary poetic ingenuity, names like "Order of Livonian Knights" appeal to the imagination, and there is an added hint of fanaticism. The phrase "Teutonic Knights" is different: those two words possess a massive, reckless power fearsome as a steamroller. The patronymics of those Teutonic Knights, such as von Salza, surname of the Order's grand master, have a ruthless ring. Von Salza, hardly a Germanic name, has exotic, barbaric associations. Similarly, the Battle of Tannenberg, which ended in the Slavs' victory over the Germanic command in 1410 and firmly halted its advance towards the east, resonates in a solemn, implacable way. Tannenberg represented one hell of a drubbing. It would seem that this name scarred the German memory, because in 1914, when Russian troops were routed after having been drawn into a trap near the Mazurian lakes, Ludendorff pleaded with Wilhelm II that his victory be given the name Tannenberg, so as to avenge the rout of 1410.

Joëlle has decided not to come to the castle with me. I sense she is a bit "oversaturated". This business about Gambia and Tobago has whetted my curiosity. That a small country in the north of Europe, isolated and barely sovereign – the duchy was indirectly dependant on the King of Poland from 1561 – should have been able to attempt such an exploit is truly miraculous. Courland, which also included the province of Zemgale, was scarcely larger than Brittany (27,000 square kilometres).

What could one do with a population of barely 200,000 inhabitants?

Jacob Kettler, Duke of Courland, was one of the rare seventeenth-century princes to take a strong interest in commerce and industry. Having travelled in Europe in his youth, he had observed its economic systems. One particular nation, Holland, had caught his attention: the inhabitants of this small state, motivated by a spirit of enterprise, displayed audacity and excelled at finding new markets for their goods. This was the model Kettler wished to implement in Courland.

The streets of Ventspils are wide and well spaced. A clear, piercing light and a salty breeze suggest proximity to the sea, yet it is not visible. As in all port cities, there is a sense of accessibility, the hint of insidious temptation. I can understand Stendhal's jubilation when he wrote of his "happiness in walking proudly through a foreign city in which I have arrived one hour ago and where I feel sure that nobody knows me . . ."

Bristling with scaffolding, Ventspils' castle is undergoing serious repair work. I come across the Professor and his wife contemplating the restoration with puzzled expressions. He, always elegant, but in a detached, casual (very un-Prussian) way, in striking contrast to his meticulous, almost inflexible manner. She, with her buxom, disgruntled, slightly faded beauty, but spirited and not at all in thrall to her husband.

The roofs have been ripped off. All that remains are the walls and the tower, redolent of the nineteenth century. What will emerge from this rubble once the cranes and scaffolding have been removed? One senses an enthusiasm and an obsessive preoccupation with reconstruction that do not augur well. In France, we are very familiar with castles like this one and with outrageously modernized buildings, "brand old" as the Professor amusingly calls them. "The Latvians have the right to repeat all of our mistakes. It may even be essential that they do so. Of course, what happens to us will give them time to consider their options. But a young nation doesn't care about the experience of old countries like ours. She wants to test everything for herself. That's what's exciting for all these former Soviet-bloc states: trying out things for themselves, losing their way, taking the same paths we took, making the same mistakes, only to arrive at the same conclusions." He bursts out laughing when I quote this *mot* of Roland Dorgelès': "Experience is like toothpicks: no-one wants to use them after you have."

The castle's position overlooking the mouth of the Venta is magnificent. The effect of the wind and the river loop is like an imperious summons to the open sea and distant lands. Yet there is nothing majestic about this small coastal river. It could be compared with the Charente in France, a waterway modest in appearance but which was used by Colbert to launch a good many of the ships in Louis XIV's fleet. The Venta's far bank, crammed with warehouses, is barely a stone's throw away.

We walk along a footpath beside the river. Sculptures along the way almost exclusively depict cows. Apparently this is the emblem the current mayor, Aivars Lembergs, chose for his city. The Professor seems fascinated by Lembergs, a former member of the Communist Party who has become one of the country's richest businessmen. He has made Ventspils the beacon of Courland, largely eclipsing its rival, Liepaja. Free of ice throughout the year, the port has always been a coveted strategic point on the Baltic. When it was part of the Soviet empire, Ventspils boasted the largest oil terminal in the USSR. Much of the crude destined for European and American markets passed through this ancient Hanseatic port.

Ventspils is linked with a controversial figure, Armand Hammer, the type of man with whom our age regularly falls in love only to erase all memory of him, not without a certain ingratitude, after his death. It is almost as if such an individual had never existed. Nicknamed the "Red Millionaire" by the French press, Hammer made a fortune after the Bolshevik Revolution, thanks to a barter scheme with the Soviets: American wheat in exchange for furs, timber and precious stones. Having invested in a moribund company, Occidental Petroleum, in 1956, he went on to turn it into the seventh-largest oil consortium in the United States. In 1972 he signed a then astronomical $20 million deal with the USSR to provide large-scale deliveries of phosphates and fertilizers. A vast trans-shipment complex for chemical goods was created at Ventspils that would guarantee the port a level of prosperity unrivalled in Latvia.

Ventspils should erect a statue to Hammer, the father of the Courland port. From Lenin to Gorbachev, the millionaire continued to have access to the Kremlin. On his death in 1990, this great art collector, who also gave financial backing to the American Republican Party, endowed a splendid museum that bears his name.

I don't know where the Professor picked it up, but he hands me a pamphlet about Ventspils, written in French. It dates from 1985, when Latvia was still Communist. With its old-fashioned layout, the brochure is delightfully Soviet in style.

We sit down on a bench. While the Professor's wife examines one of the mayor's idolized cows, I leaf through the pamphlet. The photographs, which are the colour of boiled sweets, depict the statue of Lenin and the Lenin Bridge, as well as memorials to the heroes of Labour. The contents adopt the Communist phraseology that was still in use. It is all very simple: as long as Ventspils remained within the Russian sphere of influence, everything was fine. Even the tsarist period is described indulgently. "After the introduction of the bourgeois regime in Latvia" – that is to say when the country became independent between the two world wars – everything deteriorated, however. The port entered the doldrums; the town became impoverished. After the Second World War, of course, once Latvia was under the jurisdiction of the Soviet Union once more, Ventspils experienced an unprecedented boom thanks to the construction of the Djouba (Friendship) pipeline, and thanks, too, to the trans-shipping of chemical products (ammonia, methane) and the creation of the fishermen's *kolkhoz* called Sarkana Baka (Red Lighthouse).

I suggest continuing along the river, but the Professor informs me that he has arranged to meet one of his old Latvian friends: "He works at the town hall. I think you will find him interesting."

A thickset man of about fifty comes towards us. His face, his skull, his arms – everything about him is plump. Carrying an old leather briefcase, he flops onto the bench, mopping his brow. It is immediately clear that we are dealing with a self-assured, effusive individual. The Professor and he appear to be very much in sync. Without an ounce of mockery, the Professor addresses the little man as "Hercules". I don't think this can be his real name, however.

"So, how are you finding Aivars Lembergs' city?" Hercules asks cheerfully. "I myself have nothing bad to say about him: in fact, I work for him. I can confirm that he is a good boss. Look at these streets, these pavements, the façades of those buildings, these gardens, this lawn; it's all fresh and tidy. Lembergs has transformed Ventspils. He knew what had to be done right from the beginning. The astonishing thing is that he behaves as if he were the new man, whereas it was the Communists who put him in charge of the Council in 1988. He's very clever. He'll go far, but he's got lots of enemies in Riga."

Hercules has chosen to speak in German, thus allowing the Professor to express all the fine distinctions of the conversation. Vaguely camphorated whiffs of iodine blow in on the sea breeze, together with those hints of jute and bitumen characteristic of port cities. These smells are very pleasant because they are accompanied by gusts of fresh air. The fibreglass cow lends the scene a comical dimension. We ask Hercules whether the choice of the cow as an emblem has any significance. He asserts that Lembergs' strength lies precisely in not asking oneself this type of question.

"But that doesn't stop his choice from having a meaning. Perhaps, subconsciously, he wants his staff to be like cows? Cows are, after all, animals that obediently follow the herd. The herd instinct always favours politicians, but they still have to know how to drive the cattle. He's chosen a good symbol, your mayor. We moo, we grow fat, we look without seeing, only to end up in the abattoir!"

It is not Hercules who is speaking but Louise, the Professor's wife. Her husband translates in a reproving tone of voice. Hercules bursts out laughing, and his small frame quivers: "Yes, yes, that's quite right! We are very much like cows! But I am sure that cows loathe us. I imagine that they have no worse insult than to call one another human!"

The Professor concurs: "It's odd, you French have made the cow an example of spitefulness, whereas there is no more peaceable animal." Unwisely, I ask him to give some examples. "*Peau de vache*; *vachard*; *coup de pied en vache*."* One has to admit that, without ever having been to France, the Professor, contrary to what I thought initially, knows all the nuances of French slang and colloquialisms.

He translates imperturbably, like a sort of match referee who is at the same time engrossed in correctly applying the rules. He has

144

this inimitable way of not getting involved at the heart of things while refusing to compromise about shades of meaning. For him, every word possesses a colouring that has to be conveyed by using a multitude of other words. The Professor has a control of silence so remarkable that you have the feeling he is elsewhere, that he has not understood and, above all, that he is holding back. In rhetoric, they call this aposiopesis. His abrupt way of interrupting a phrase with a blank resembling a reprimand sometimes creates moments of awkwardness and uncertainty, which he enjoys dispelling in his own way, occasionally overdoing it. Observing the concern and then the relief that we exhibit affords him genuine delight.

Following the Dutch example, then, the Duke of Courland invested in shipbuilding. Hercules points out the likely site of the shipyards: an island to the south, on a bend in the Venta. As yet, no trace of the installations has been found. According to him, almost 150 ships were built there. Some were sold abroad, notably to France. Duke Jacob was in negotiations with the French to purchase the port of Marennes, in the Charente, but the talks collapsed because of the war with Sweden.*

I peppered Hercules with questions about Tobago and Saint Andrews, the island off Gambia. Why had the small Duchy of Courland embarked upon such expeditions? "It's very simple," Hercules said fluently. "Duke Jacob was an adventurer. I think he was slightly mad, and, like all madmen, he had a rational side. He realized that a country is defined by its natural resources and the need to produce a range of manufactured goods. Very early on, he favoured foreign trade over domestic consumption. In the area of shipbuilding, which he organized on the Dutch model – the seventeenth-century benchmark – his yards produced everything from rigging to sails, masts, tar, guns, saltpetre and gunpowder. As far as metal fittings were concerned –

145

nails, anchors, chains, weaponry – Courland lacked the necessary raw materials, so the Duke bought up iron-ore deposits in Norway. A large number of manufactured goods were exported. At heart, he was an entrepreneur. Convinced of the superiority of foreign items such as glassware, tapestry, jewellery and leather goods, he never stopped producing them, intending to eliminate the domestic market and compete with the outside world. There was only one essential thing he could not manufacture, and that was spices. And so, lacking neither courage nor a fanciful turn of mind, he embarked upon his faraway adventures. Several attempts at colonization had already taken place in 1638 and 1642, but it was only in May 1654 that the two-decker *Duchess of Courland* weighed anchor from the spot where we are standing now. Imagine the scene on this small river. It is probable that the ship, like Dutch oceangoing vessels, had a shallow draught, because of the numerous sandbanks in the Baltic and North seas. There can be no doubt that, for such a distant destination, a flat-bottomed ship would have carried its sails better and pitched less at sea."

Hercules inhales sea air through his powerful nostrils, as if calling on us to witness or imitate the scene that took place here over three centuries ago. Unlike everyone else we have met, he gesticulates constantly while speaking. There is something fiery about him, a sociable, childlike quality, as well as an astonishing serenity. You feel that his nerve-batteries switch off instantly, whereas his countrymen stiffen at first contact. His enthusiasm is a joy to behold.

Like other Latvians of his age, Hercules has lived through a traumatic experience, a major assault: the occupation of his country. How did he manage to endure the Soviet system, with its inevitable dishonourable solutions? He appears unscathed, harbours no resentment and is free of cynicism. What does he get up to at the town hall with the extremely controversial Lembergs? Hercules comes across as one of those innocent creatures who witness history's cruelties without ever being affected by them. "Each of us lived in his own hideaway," he says almost apologetically.

Between him and the Professor there is an understanding moderated on occasion by the German's jibes, if one can judge by a taunting tone in his voice. How did they come to know one another? Normally, I do not have the least compunction about asking questions that might seem indiscreet, but the Professor, without appearing aloof, always reacts with an absence of emotion that can seem like coldness. Yet he is not lacking in occasional sensitivity, even enthusiasm. His equanimity clearly irritates his wife, a mercurial character, impatient and rebellious, who tends to be more practical. She regards Hercules with almost motherly affection, from time to time straightening his ghastly polyester tie.

I have still not asked the Professor about how he came to learn Latvian. Their linguistic asides lead me to think that Hercules had something to do with it.

THE COURLAND CAP

Is it the mention of Tobago and the tropics? Or the feeling of having penetrated a secret intimacy, as if I were trying to fathom someone's weakness? As a distraction, I have a sudden desire, this afternoon, to smoke a cigar, a ritual I usually save for the evening. Hercules watches me light up with amusement. "The wind is going to smoke the cigar instead of you," the Professor says disapprovingly. I point out that there is no wind and that this halt by the river's mouth is conducive to enjoyment and, more than anything else, an exercise in meditation: "Don't you feel that the water here appears to be gathering its strength before it plunges into the sea? Hercules could not have chosen a better place to remind us of the *Duchess of Courland* weighing anchor. This spot marks a pause before the pitch into the churning ocean."

But I am hardly going to recite the opening verses of Rimbaud's *Le Bateau ivre*! The Professor looks somewhat put out. He is not used to seeing me like this, elated by imperturbable rivers . . .

The slate-grey waters streaming by possess a voice. We can hear it speaking through Hercules' baritone, relayed meticulously by the Professor. There is a huge contrast between the solemn, emotional tone of the one and the monotone echo produced by the other. Hercules is rather like a medium. He *sees* the scene: the ship slipping down the Venta, armed with its forty-five guns. On board the *Duchess of Courland*, which is captained by a Dutchman, are twenty-five officers, a hundred and eighty soldiers and, of particular significance, eighty

Courland families who have opted for a tropical adventure. Had the Courland colonizers, like the passengers aboard the *Mayflower*, signed a pact before they left, in which the principles of their communal life were inscribed? Hercules says that virtually nothing is known of their histories. What *is* known is that Tobago was christened New Courland, and that the land there was divided into plots. The Courland pioneers built the fort at Jekabforts, as well as a town, Jekaba Pilseta (Jamestown).

This settlement must have survived for about forty years. The island was eventually handed over to the British. In 1813, a traveller drew attention to the existence of 12,000 settlers in Tobago: Dutch, French Huguenots and Courlanders. Hercules points out that there is still a Courland Bay in Tobago. A memorial was even unveiled there in 1975, in the presence of descendants of the last dukes.

Hercules feels a naïve desire to re-enact the departure scene, as if to suggest that in leaving Windau, the passengers aboard the *Duchess of Courland* were starting again from scratch, far from the corruption of Old Europe. He develops an entire theory about commitment and challenge. To cope with the distance and separation, strong inducements were required. Gaston Bachelard maintains that "the really powerful interests are fanciful interests". Is what we dream of ultimately more effective than what we calculate? "It was essentially the lure of money that guided them," the Professor says. Hercules does not agree. They argue for a while, the Professor not deigning to translate his friend's remarks. A little later, he takes me aside and says, "They're very gullible, these Latvians. They believe in the myth of America, the 'frontier'. Hercules takes the story of the Promised Land at face value. If you think about it, American civilization has only produced worse property slaves than those in Europe, a Puritanism that is far more insidious than in our Lutheran countries and a cult of violence successfully passed on to us through their cinema." A simplistic view; Tobago has nothing to do with the American prairie. "It's a colonial adventure, nonetheless," the Professor says, bringing the conversation to an abrupt conclusion.

Our heated discussions beside the river have caught the attention of passers-by. I am sitting on the bench with Louise, with Hercules and the Professor circling us repeatedly, varying their pace according to the rhythm of their exchanges and the intensity of the conversation. Other walkers are amused to see me smoking a cigar. I have noticed elsewhere this curiosity that prevents me from fully enjoying a Havana. The river's murky waters bubble as they meet the bank, while leaves and twigs in midstream flow victoriously towards the sea.

I have the feeling that the Professor has inhibited Hercules' momentum. He replies elliptically to our questions about Gambia, Courland's other colonial adventure.

A small group has formed about a hundred metres from our bench. Hercules' expression changes abruptly. "The mayor ... He's coming towards us." A small man with intelligent, inquisitive eyes, wearing a large hat and possessed of an uncertain manner, walks over. As soon as he spots Hercules, his suspicious and awkward attitude vanishes. Once introductions have been made, he flushes and adopts a kindly expression bordering on naiveté. Nevertheless, one senses his contained nervous energy, a quick and shifty way of sizing up the person he is talking to so as to assess his *"tirant d'eau"*, as Napoleon used to say. The mayor jokes with Hercules for a few moments. He seems fascinated by my cigar. "Ventspils, it's the city of the future," Aivars Lembergs says before disappearing.

I am slightly disappointed: he could have come up with a more original slogan. It appears that he often quotes a saying of Duke Jacob's which, he believes, characterizes the mentality of Courlanders: "We neither have friends in the East nor in the West. We have only interests." This character, one of the wealthiest oligarchs in the land, is obviously far shrewder than he appears. It is clear that he understands human nature completely.

These exchanges have lasted no more than two minutes. Hercules seems proud of the mayor's performance: "He goes about on foot; he is very close to the people and makes up his own mind about everything. Thanks to him, Ventspils has an international Olympic centre and one of the cleanest beaches in the Baltic. That's quite an achievement when one realizes that the sea is one of the most polluted in Europe. An artificial ski slope has been built; the people call it 'Lembergs's hat'. The mayor's hat has become a symbol! He works very hard. He didn't even ask me why I was not at my desk. He trusts his people." The most suspicious politician could not fail to trust a man like Hercules, who exudes integrity and takes everything literally.

When I toss my Havana's remains into the river, Hercules stares after it in amazement. This reminds me of a scene described by Stendhal: "I threw my cigar in the Loire, in an apparently ridiculous gesture of respect, for the old women stared at me." We gaze fondly at the butt of my Havana. It floats on the current, becomes saturated and disappears into a swirl. This brief voyage of a half-smoked cigar has deeply impressed Hercules. The *Duchess of Courland* would have sunk before his eyes in the same way had he looked half as astonished. For a long time he remains lost in thought. Then, pulling himself together as if nothing has happened, he begins to talk about Gambia, the very subject which, a few moments ago, caused him to sulk.

It so happens that I passed through Gambia about thirty years ago while on an assignment in Senegal. This tiny strip of land can only be passed through; it is usually compared to one finger of a glove. Gambia is situated on both sides of the river of the same name, which I remember as princely, majestic and impenetrable, with a tangle of tributaries and a few islands near its mouth. It was on one of these that the Courlanders who had sailed from Windau landed in 1651. According to Hercules, it was Tobago that justified the settlement in Gambia. In order to exploit the plantations on his West Indian island, Jacob Kettler needed to import slaves. He wrote to Innocent X, proposing a partnership: the Pope would supply the financing, Kettler the boats and men. The project was on the point of succeeding when Innocent X died. Although all of the Duke of Courland's plans collapsed, he did not admit defeat, despatching two ships, the *Whale* and the *Crocodile*, to West Africa. These ships having found the mouth of a river, it was decided to sail up it. The expedition landed on an island situated about thirty kilometres inland. It was christened Saint-André. A fortress was built and given the name Jacobus.

"See what the Courlanders did! There's an imaginative toughness to our people, an organizational sense that occasionally inspires them to overcome insurmountable obstacles."

"Insurmountable, but these men were motivated by self-interest more than anything else. That island was used as a base for the slave trade. After all, *Kettler* in German means 'chain-maker'."

The Professor is never easily taken in. Hercules has the look of a pupil who has been caught out but who has no intention of apologizing.

"You're right, but you have to put his behaviour into context. Other ships brought more Courland colonizers after this first expedition. There were twenty or more voyages. The Courlanders were the first to evangelize in Black Africa. I've worked on the archives of this period. Blacks were even brought back to Courland. Imagine the curiosity those Africans must have aroused here! I've discovered the story of a certain Kotus, a kind of African noble who caused a sensation at the court of Duke Jacob. He was a giant, a fine figure of a man, curious about but not surprised by anything. Having never seen snow before, he desperately wanted to take some back to his country, though he understood that it melted in the heat. We shall never know what happened to him, which for me is the most exciting part of the story. Kotus returned home. He must have related the account of his journey. One can imagine that the tale of his adventures would have been transmitted orally over several generations. It's not impossible: traces never disappear completely. Remember *Roots*, that American best-seller by Alex Haley? Haley managed to trace his ancestors, who had probably set sail from Saint-André, which, up until the nineteenth century, was one of the most important centres of the slave trade in Africa.

"It was in 1661 that the English took over the fortress; the island changed its name to St James. The Duke of Courland's expansionist adventure was fairly short-lived. The enterprise was beyond his means; he was obstinate, he had ambition, but it was too limited, and his foreign policy lacked consistency. Woe to small nations, especially when they live in the shadow of large ones! That was Courland's problem, and it's Latvia's problem today."

"The Latvians love to say that they are a small country. Such false modesty becomes irritating in the long run. Denmark, Switzerland, Holland, Belgium – they all have far smaller surface areas. So, why this inferiority complex? It's as if you don't want to let yourselves be seen outside your borders. All countries project an image, real or invented, to the outside world. Except for you Latvians. You feel comfortable in your isolation. I wonder whether it's not a form of pride. You are very

153

much on your own. Estonia is tied to Finland, Lithuania to Poland. Latvia has no-one but herself. In short, you haven't any friends."

"That's the Russians' fault! They don't like us. They control Latvia's image. They portray us as bad Europeans, as people who do not respect the rights of minorities. They are very powerful; we are so weak!"

"That's quite enough! Do you think you're helping yourselves by turning yourselves into victims?"

To avoid another squabble, I suggest that we continue our walk in the direction of the historical centre, where restoration work is in full swing: the clanging of cranes, the clatter of scaffolding boards, the drone of pneumatic drills can all be heard from far away.

Adorned with lambrequins, the old wooden houses have had a facelift. Pavements, shops and frontages that had already done their time by the 1960s have held out to their absolute limit, have endured until their very substance was at breaking point. Disintegration was imminent. We are witnessing a miracle, even though the authorities' hands have been vigorously forced in order to achieve it.

An imposing statue on a street corner arouses my curiosity: a man proudly standing his ground, dressed in a three-quarter-length coat, his left hand gripping the pommel of an infantry sword. He wears the peaked Red Army cap, with its star. A name is inscribed on the pedestal: Janis Fabricius.

"One of the Bolshevik leaders, a colleague of Trotsky's. Fabricius played an important role in 1917 and afterwards. He came from a village south of Ventspils. A well-known Latvian sculptor of the 1950s, Janis Zarins, created this sculpture; it was awarded a Lenin Prize. It was Zarins who made the enormous statue of Lenin that overlooked the port. We had that one taken down."

I am amazed that they should have done away with the father of the Bolshevik Revolution but kept one of its leaders. Hercules explains: "The two men were quite different. Fabricius was one of us, a true Courlander. Many of the revolutionary leaders came from Courland. The anti-Communists have never trusted us. According to them, the Bolshevik pox spread through Latvia via the ports of Liepaja and Ventspils. This statue is part of our city's folklore. On 24 June, the festival of Ligo, which was suppressed under the Communist regime, the crowd used to crown Fabricius with oak leaves."

One cannot think too badly of such a statue, even if, given its Social Realist style, it represents a menacing aspect of revolution-on-the-march. I feel a particular affection for the Red Army cap with its conical peak. To me, this headgear, a legacy of the caps worn by Budienny's cavalry, is enchanting. I suddenly realize why: the cap is the same shape as Courland itself. I share this discovery with my companions: "Of course the statue of Fabricius will never be removed: it has Courland on its head!"

They regard me as if I were out of my mind. The Professor looks up at Fabricius's head and then, rather cruelly, examines my own. Instantly, his expression softens: "Our friend is right. Fabricius's cap does indeed resemble Courland. How incredible! Look at its peak: it's Cape Kolka. Obviously, it's a bit worn away, for that strip of land is continually being eroded by the Baltic . . ." Hercules maintains that the pointed tip of the Red Army's headgear proved very useful in cold weather. "Courland actually looks more like an Ottoman beret," he says. I point out that they are similar shapes. "A cap," he says, "but who is wearing it? Where's the head? Where's the face? Anyway, it's unkind to compare my country to a hat!"

ROMANTIC COURLAND

Our last meal with the Professor and his wife; their ferry is departing at midnight. Hercules joins us for dinner at the hotel. His garrulousness and cheerful manner help to dispel the melancholy of departure. Shall we see our friends again? The Professor promises to come to France to learn about our great vintages and to benefit, he says, from my advice.

"A German can't abide the French; yet he happily drinks their wines.'"

"Don't you like us?"

"I thought I had proved that I do in the past few days. The phrase is not mine but Goethe's. I hope you will send a copy of your article to us in Germany. I am keen to read your impressions."

"You'll be disappointed. The most interesting part of this journey, which I owe to our meeting, has to be made to disappear. That's the paradox inherent in this type of journalism: you have to conceal the essence, that is to say the unexpected, the surprises. I shall write about the past, the quality of silence, the history, a few observations about the end of Communism, all dressed up with some conventional remarks by Courlanders, which will be plentiful because that is the slant I wish to give my article. It needs to be practical, positive and slightly unreal as well. I must make the reader daydream. Fortunately, those grand houses will provide a proper dose of romanticism."

"Are they not romantic in fact? This country couldn't be more romantic."

"No doubt, but that means nothing. *Romantic's* a catch-all word.

Everything having to do with the emotions or with an attractive past is romantic. The magazine that sent me here expects sparkling stuff. The landscapes have to glisten; the buildings have to make readers reflect. It is vital that the characters be both colourful and unusual but not *too* colourful and unusual. A piece that is spuriously inspired, with the appearance of objectivity: that is what's expected of me! You know, Courland means little to the French. There's Louis XVIII's exile in Mitau, but how many people are aware that Mitau is in Courland, or rather, that it used to be?"*

"You'll like Mitau, but make sure to see Blankenfeld too. Nobody mentions that grand house where Louis XVIII lived. It hasn't changed, whereas Mitau was badly damaged during the First World War and virtually destroyed in 1944, during the Second."

Hercules interrupts to point out that the front line at the time ran along the railway line from Mitau to Liepaja. This reference to the war makes me think of the Resurrector. I have left him several messages to no avail. The most frustrating thing is that that Hercules knows him. He welcomed him to Ventspils' town hall to discuss formalities having to do with his excavations.

The Courland Pocket has made a deep impression. On V.E. Day, 8 May, 1945, two convoys organized by the *Kriegsmarine* succeeded in escaping from the port of Ventspils. On board were 11,500 German soldiers who managed to get back to the ports of Holstein, whereas almost 200,000 troops marooned in Courland surrendered to the Soviet army, among them the commander-in-chief, General Hilpert, who died in a concentration camp. Of those 200,000 Germans, sent for the most part to Siberia, only 10,000 would return.

This period inspired intense discussions between Hercules and the Professor which were translated for me all too hastily. When I complained about this, the Professor explained that they were arguing about the German–Soviet Treaty of 1939. The Molotov–Ribbentrop Pact included a secret protocol: in return for the annexation of western Poland by Germany, the Soviets would be given the Baltic countries and eastern Poland. Up until 22 June, 1941 – the launch of Operation Barbarossa – Latvia endured the harsh Communist yoke, along with arrests and deportations.

The debate between the two men has to do with the arrival of the German troops, who were greeted as liberators by the Latvian people. "It's easy to make judgements today. People did not know about the secret stipulations in the German–Soviet Treaty. They thought that the Wehrmacht had come to save them. They quickly realized their mistake." In an aside, the Professor confides, "The Second World War is a sensitive subject here; the Latvians don't like talking about it much. It's a scar on the collective memory." Hercules has not understood, but he is no fool: "During the Soviet period, we watched too many propaganda films about the war, featuring good Russians and wicked Germans."

I did not realize that the clauses in the 1939 treaty, long kept secret by the Soviets, had played a part in Latvia's progress towards independence. In August 1987, on the treaty's anniversary, there were widespread demonstrations. The following year, the authorities in Moscow finally decided to publish details of the stipulations, recognizing implicitly the errors of Stalin's regime. This admission, with perestroika in full swing, hastened the process of self-determination.

On 23 August, 1989, a unique event took place. Fifty years after the signing of the Molotov–Ribbentrop Pact, a human chain made up of people from the three Baltic nations stretched over 600 kilometres, from Tallinn to Vilnius, via Riga.

At a table close to ours, some Courland yuppies – ultra-flat mobile phones, black polo necks, meticulously shaved heads – are talking loudly and drinking organic cucumber juice. They have a cold, seductive look, and the same impatient arrogance as our young sharks in France.

Even though we are being discreet and avoiding their gaze, our vibes have probably made them aware that we've been talking about them. I have often noticed this phenomenon among people who do not speak French, though I imagine it can be observed everywhere. It only requires speech rhythms to decrease, and voices to drop, for the modulation to attract attention. Whereas in France we pretend not to notice and raise our voices still louder, our young parvenus grow quieter, only to subside entirely, regarding their plates gloomily. Our financial dandies still have some way to go . . . They are a bit too soft, perhaps, to be true, arrogant Europeans. The French have nicknamed a certain category of well-off, eager and not very amusing middle-class youth "*bobolsheviks*". This description suits our neighbours perfectly.

The Professor raises his glass to toast our health – I chose a Beaujolais from the wine list to please him. He maintains that this is French wine par excellence. To be honest, we could have fared worse: it is fruity and easy to drink. The Professor even uses the word *lively*, a term I loathe, but it is the accepted adjective for describing this type of wine. Where did he pick it up?

Hercules is clearly enjoying this typically French product, so we order a second bottle. The Professor is moved. Declaring that the "fermentation of fate" brought about our meeting, he develops an entire theory about our initial encounter at Laidi, which had no immediate repercussions. That occasion feels so far away now that I find it hard to believe that it happened only a week ago. According to the

Professor, fermentation was already beginning; it would determine the events of that night, when Joëlle got out of bed to examine the little girl who was ill. "We expropriated fate," the Professor bangs on. Yes, why not? His wife regards him angrily. Could he be slightly drunk? At the start of the meal, he knocked back two vodkas in quick succession, which is quite unlike him.

This man is a mystery. Since we first met, he has given away little about himself. He has been the ideal travelling companion, in possession of a perceptive intelligence, positive, hugely knowledgeable, a bit stiff in his manner (which can verge on coldness), exhausting yet discriminating, and with that superior nonchalance that cannot be acquired but which thoroughly irritates those around him. So I find it hard to understand the feelings he arouses in his wife. I believe she appreciates his intellectual qualities; as for his moral ones, I'm not so sure. She fails to disguise a sort of resentment towards him.

We accompany them to the ferry. A long line of trucks is waiting in the night. Everything is brightly lit by floodlights and spotlights atop bridge-like derricks. People seem to be dressed in their best; the port is bathed in an atmosphere of festivity. The procession of goods lorries and caravans, interspersed with motorcycles, their headlights full on, resembles a parade of floats and outriders. The blare of intermingled music from car radios simultaneously creates a holiday mood and one of regret. All these vehicles are leaving; their occupants have come to the end of their stay.

As I watch the Professor's car disappear, I have the sense that for me, too, the party is over.

A final vision of Louise drying her eyes with one hand and waving to us with the other.

The Professor looks as if he is about to explode with fury.

THE VENUS OF BLANKENFELD

Blankenfeld is at the end of the world. The mansion is hidden away in a hamlet close to the Lithuanian border. We have not encountered a single other car for miles. From a distance, the building, whose long, low outline is reminiscent of a Bordelais charterhouse, is not unattractive. Entry is through a portico with four small columns in the Tuscan style.

A woman holding a bunch of large keys awaits us on the steps. Just as I am thinking that we will have to content ourselves with admiring the building's exterior, her gestures give us to understand – she speaks only Latvian – that we may go inside. An attempt has been made to make the rooms into a museum by exhibiting mouldings and cornices in one and a collection of ploughs in another. A chipped plate, an assortment of rusty nails . . . these objects appear to be of no interest. The collection is based purely on the principles of accumulation and stacking. The hotchpotch is impressive in that it possesses a sense of resoluteness and a longevity acquired over centuries.

Museography is a passion among the Courlanders. The most humble village, the smallest country house, has its cabinet of curiosities, often quite modest, crammed with unlikely objects. The most extraordinary one I visited displayed a complete collection of saws dating from the Communist period, an array rich in lessons about the Soviet objective: its primitive, resolute, dull side, as well as a perpetually worrying weirdness.

Throw nothing away, hand everything on at all costs, indiscriminately, to ensure that it will still be there for future generations. Is this anxiety symptomatic of a land still feeling its way while reconstructing its past?

The woman, who is about forty, follows us from one room to the other, jangling her keys. She looks like a peasant; her sullen face wears a rather irritating, shifty expression. What is astonishing is how perfect her features are. This key-bearer with the sulky demeanour is a real beauty. Not one of those dazzling, photogenic Venuses who make your head turn in the street, but a queen of the night with inscrutable charm. The kind of looks you are unaware of to begin with, whose perfection, only gradually revealed, can be deceiving. But there's a problem: you realize straight away that there is nothing behind this faultless façade, no grace, no sensitivity, merely harshness and a calculating manner that dispels attraction.

I cannot stop gazing at her, contemplating this living contradiction, the warden of an empty museum. How many visitors has she encountered? Who would think of exploring such a place unless they were admirers of Louis XVIII? There is nothing to recall the exiled king's stay here, apart from a poor reproduction of a painting by Gérard (in this best-known portrait of the monarch, the artist depicted him in his office at the Tuileries).

Not a single mention of the circumstances in which the banished king came to live in this house at the beginning of his second stay in Courland, in 1804, before he moved to Mitau. I imagine him in this back-of-beyond hole, being welcomed by the Königsfelds, a family of the Germano-Baltic aristocracy. This shack, with its fibro-cement roof, is just as sad as Longwood, Napoleon's last home. It gives off the same smell: a stench of mildew and poverty, a whiff of old boots and moth-eaten fur that I associate with oblivion and exile. This place, which resembles an old convent, is worse than Saint Helena. Throughout the whole of Louis XVIII's wanderings, "there were no hours more painful than those he spent at Blankenfeld", Ernest Daudet would write later.* The only difference is that the Bourbon king has never appealed to the imagination. There is no comparison between a legendary character such as Napoleon and this sickly king who was usually rooted to his chair by gout.

I don't know whether these rooms were laid out in the same way in Louis XVIII's day; given their outmoded appearance, there is no reason to think they have been altered very much. In a place like this, you had to believe firmly in your own good fortune. A single relic arouses my curiosity: a photograph apparently taken from the park.

Few great country houses display mementos of their former owners. This is due as much to a lack of documentation or keepsakes, I imagine, as to a vague animosity on the part of the local population towards aristocrats who left bad memories behind, memories of a class disinclined to share their wealth and whose privileges cut them off from others. "Courland: the paradise of the nobility and the hell of the peasantry", to quote an eighteenth-century traveller, Baron von Blomberg.† This antipathy has no doubt diminished in the memory of Courlanders, who increasingly regard such architectural assets as belonging to the heritage of their province.

The photograph depicts a meal being eaten in the shade of some trees. The women look at the camera with a triumphant air bordering on insolence. The men, gazing sideways, wear astonished expressions. The date: 1913, the last flickerings of happiness before the apocalypse. This image is hauntingly reminiscent of Keyserling's novels: nobody knows what is about to happen, but the menace is there. (Speaking of which, it is significant that Courland pays no attention to this writer, who was born at the manor of Padure, near the small town of Aizpute; only one of his novels, *Bunte Herzen*, has recently been translated into Latvian.)

The bearer of the keys invites us round to the rear of the house. The veranda looks out onto the park, or what remains of it. Crimson seats rather like those in theatres or cinemas have been set out to either side. I wonder whether this house was not a hospice at one time, but how can one find out?

The warden gives us to understand that our visit is over; there is nothing more to see. Placing herself in front of us, she adopts a modest, begging stance. A human expression suffuses her beautiful face. She expects a tip. We would not dream of contesting what is her due; this was no ordinary visit. Thanks to her, Blankenfeld was worth going out of our way for. We say goodbye. She still does not smile but timidly gestures to us to stop. What does she want? Her words are incomprehensible.

She picks up her bag, switches off the lights, locks the front door. I think I understand what she is trying to say: she wants a lift. Joëlle and I look at one another in a quandary. The woman mentions the name of the neighbouring village and begins to smile. Her expression, more of a grimace, does not suit her. I prefer her surly face.

We leave her at the outskirts of the village, by a bus stop.

A final image of the Courland Venus, standing motionless: her impenetrable face gives her the appearance of a deity carved in marble.

MADAME ROYALE'S TREE

On 28 March, 1799, Louis XVIII, the wandering monarch, driven out of Blankenburg in the Duchy of Brunswick by the Prussians, arrived at Mitau. A Russian guard of honour was waiting to present arms and greet him in a dignified manner. Throughout his wanderings, accepting the hospitality and charity of European princes – his "cousins" – such pomp and ceremony were liable to affect him. But he was not a man to display or experience emotion. Mitau reminded him of Versailles. He had not set eyes on France since that day in 1791 when he had fled to Koblenz.

It would not be long before the king realized that the magnificence of Mitau was merely a trompe l'oeil. Inside the palace, which had more than 300 rooms, there was nothing. Only the apartment assigned to him was vaguely inhabitable. The great event during this first period of exile in Courland, which would end in 1801, was the marriage of the Duc d'Angoulême to his cousin, Marie-Thérèse of France, better known as Madame Royale: the prisoner in the Temple, Louis XVI's daughter, the family's only survivor.

After a further period spent wandering through Poland and Sweden, the pretender to the throne would stay at Mitau again from 1804 to 1807, after a stop at Blankenfeld. This second visit was even gloomier than the first, and God knows the first one was not exactly jolly! But Louis XVIII was unruffled. Nothing got him down. Like Napoleon – it is something they had in common – he trusted to luck.

How could fortune fail him? It was etched in his name, in his ancient race, in divine law.

On the death of Louis XVII in 1795, he had relinquished the title of Comte de Provence to become Louis XVIII, King of France and Navarre, in accordance with dynastic custom. He ruled for four years, far from his kingdom, of course, but as its legitimate monarch. Not for one moment did he consider relinquishing his rights and his royal prerogative. His conviction that he would return to rule at the Tuileries one day showed admirable certainty when one thinks of his twenty-three years spent as a wanderer and the circumstances surrounding that return in 1814, which were uncertain, to say the least.

An egoist and a dissembler, Louis XVIII has never aroused sympathy, but of all the arrogant, frequently mediocre émigrés scattered throughout Germany, England, Austria and Russia, his was without a doubt one of the most perceptive minds, in any case the most realistic, as he would demonstrate at the time of the first Restoration by signing the constitutional Charter preceded by the Proclamation of Saint-Ouen.* He was a true politician, unlike his brother, the shallow and not very bright Comte d'Artois.†

I had imagined Louis XVIII's chateau to be lost in open countryside. Hidden away in the heart of the city, it arouses a sense of astonishment once you find it. It is a veritable palace, in fact, a large quadrilateral, grandiose without being overwhelming. Exterior decoration is confined to pilasters and the contrast between red roughcast walls and white stucco window frames and ledges. There is something spellbinding about this pervasive ox-blood colour. It gives the scene a weird, almost supernatural aspect, evoking fire and something secretive and nocturnal, a state of suspension, as if this palace defied the laws of gravity, not that there is anything light or airy about it. And yet what grace, what sophistication there is in this display of stone and colour designed by an architect of Italian origin, Bartolomeo Rastrelli, born in Paris in 1700, "the last representative of the great European Baroque"!* It is to him that we owe, most notably, the Winter Palace in St Petersburg, which houses the Hermitage Museum, as well as the Smolny Convent and Tsarskoye Selo Palace. One feels a sense of unreality, of fear almost, on approaching such an ineffable object.

Our footsteps echo on the paving stones of the vast, deserted inner courtyard. There is a touch of Versailles about this building. Nothing of the *Grand Siècle*, however: we find ourselves, in fact, gazing at the purest and most elegant form of Russian Rococo; it is rather the barracks atmosphere that makes one think of the Sun King's palace. A dead garrison . . .

In this month of July, places have taken on an abandoned look. When you examine the building's walls closely, you can see the plaster flaking off. Security ropes prevent access to certain areas due to the danger, apparently, of falling cornices. The Rococo, one of the most original expressions of the Enlightenment . . . What a mistake it is to see this style merely as an expression of sinuousness, of profusion, when it also has to do with a kind of equilibrium, a feeling for light, an intimacy and a pliability that has been described as "the style of the joyous moment".†

There are so many ways into this palace that it is difficult to find the main entrance. In the enormous, excessively grandiose courtyard, I find myself thinking of the story the Professor told about Maurice de Saxe. When he was elected Grand Duke of Courland, Maurice decided to live at Mitau, then the duchy's capital. In order to bring some order to his life, he considered marrying the widow of his predecessor, Anna Ivanovna, who found this handsome, energetic fellow, so much younger than her, very much to her taste. Unfortunately, early one morning the widow caught him unawares, in the snowy courtyard of the ducal palace, carrying one of her maids on his shoulders, the only means of concealing her footprints and the proof that they had spent the night together.

Anna soon forgot Maurice, but she liked good-looking giants. And so it was that she fell for the charms of one of those forces of nature, Ernst-Johann de Biron, who was endowed with both great powers of seduction and a complete lack of scruples.

This adventurer's origins are uncertain; it is thought that he came from Westphalia. His name is equally vague: Bühren, Biren – he would later adopt the spelling Biron so as to suggest a relationship with the Gontaud-Biron family. As Anna Ivanovna's secretary, Ernst-Johann proved to be an excellent administrator; he also became her lover. Peter the Great's niece trusted him completely, but to keep up appearances, she arranged a marriage with one of her lady's maids, Benigna von Trotta, who would become the grandmother of the Duchess of Dino.

Ernst-Johann's other bit of luck was to coincide with the rising fortunes of his protectress, who became Empress of Russia under the name of Anne I. For ten years he was the true master of the Muscovite empire, initiating a reign of terror and confusion known as the *bironovchtchina* ("muddle *à la* Biron"). Showered with honours and riches, he never forgot his own country, however, and succeeded in having himself elected Duke of Courland in 1737 by the local nobility. The following year, he commissioned Rastrelli to build the palace of Mitau.

With the death of the empress in 1740, a time of trial began for her favourite. Even though Anna Ivanovna had appointed him Regent, Ernst-Johann fell victim to a conspiracy. Arrested and condemned to death, he narrowly escaped execution, instead being banished to

Siberia and, later, transferred to the Upper Volga. He spent twenty years in exile. Mitau was left unfinished. After many trials and tribulations, the former favourite regained his freedom, as well as his dukedom, in 1763, thanks to the new empress, Catherine II. His return meant that work on the palace at Mitau, which had been interrupted in 1740, could be completed. Ernst-Johann's son, Peter, succeeded him in 1773. After two unhappy marriages, the new duke took as his third wife Anna-Dorothea von Medem, who was thirty-seven years younger than him and belonged to one of the most illustrious and wealthiest families in Courland. Though short in stature, "the divine Anna", as she was known, was ravishingly beautiful.

Eventually we discover some steps leading up to a fairly imposing double door. Bolted. We try our luck a little further on. Padlocked.

We have to accept it: the palace of Mitau is closed. We wander along the outer walls until a shadow emerges through an opening. We rush over to the stranger, a young man whose arms are laden with folders. He makes a rapid motion with his right fist, a universal gesture: closed, locked, out of bounds. Seeing our disappointment, he puts his folders on a window-sill and explains in English that the opening of the palace has been "suspended" for an unspecified time because of falling masonry, which is a hazard to the public. He informs us that the palace now houses the agricultural university, which specializes in training for farming, forestry and food processing. To console us, he assures us that there is not much to see inside: "This palace is a fake. The two world wars destroyed 90 per cent of Jelgava [Mitau's Latvian name, apparently derived from a Livonian word]. What you see, the façades that is, is more or less original. The interior was virtually demolished by bombs. Believe me, you would find it disappointing." Virtually demolished:

everything hinges on that nuance. As far as I know, the necropolis of the dukes of Courland is still there.

As the young man picks up his folders, I can see him hesitate. Our disappointment has made him feel sorry for us. Putting his index finger to his lips as if to say, "Shhhh," he invites us into the house. There are vast corridors such as one sees in universities the world over, with noticeboards at the entrance, signposts and nameplates above the doors of the lecture halls. The place is structured like a palace, with very high ceilings and endless corridors, but nothing remains of the Rococo decor. Only the entrance hall and a few vaulted passageways have survived. A smell of chlorine and fresh sawdust lingers in the air. The silence, the stale atmosphere and the summery bleakness impart a sense of melancholy reminiscent of the monotony and gloom of the palace when it was bereft of furniture and pomp in Louis XVIII's time. It is the opposite of Saint Helena. Exiguity characterizes Longwood, the farmhouse where Napoleon lived;* Mitau is grandiose and empty. There's too much space.

I consider the French colony at Mitau, far from home. How large was it? The author of one of the best biographies of Louis XVIII, Philip Mansel,† with whom I've been in touch, has calculated that the king's entourage comprised a hundred and eight people, as well as a hundred bodyguards – though there were no more than forty-five at the time of the second visit. This figure does not include either the courtiers' servants, or the friends and relatives who accompanied each member of the royal family living with the king, or their own servants. In total, one might reasonably estimate a figure of 300 people at the time of the first emigration. Louis XVIII's small court may have been larger than Napoleon's, but it was not able to cope with the solitude. There is nothing for the eye or the imagination to grasp in all this vastness.

The mind is unable to reach any conclusion; it loses itself in emptiness. The exiled monarch said that he had accepted Mitau since there was nothing better, "just as one accepts a bed in a hospital".

What did the king do with his time? Curiously, the documentation is quite sparse. Mansel has confirmed that few reliable accounts exist about life at court or about Louis' activities.

The only historian to have studied this little-known period is Ernest Daudet, brother of Alphonse. Making use of letters and reports written by a few of those who were close to the court, he published *Histoire de l'emigration* in three volumes in 1904. Although this work is a mine of information, it is not authoritative since Daudet never cites his sources. However, he does provide details which curiously resemble those of Napoleon's existence on Saint Helena ten or so years later: the fastidious etiquette upon which the exiled king insisted, the rather pointless ceremony of mealtimes, the long evenings during which people harped on about the past, the forlorn card games, the petty intrigues.

In exile, the king led an ordered, almost monastic life. He mainly kept an eye on the movements of the complex network of informers and spies which he maintained across Europe and in France. He spent the better part of his time instructing his delegates, of whom he had far too many (and they were not exactly geniuses). The king had far more faith in the virtues of covert diplomacy than in power or making sonorous pronouncements.

Louis XVIII left nothing at Mitau: not the slightest romantic or tragic trace, not the tiniest anecdote, nothing but this dismal silence, this mundane dreariness of a university bereft of students. All this bleak decor accomplished was to reassure the claimant, for he only felt at ease when everything went like clockwork. The routine drone of etiquette immured him cosily in the "dignity of his crown".

The sorcerer Cagliostro, on the other hand, who had paid a flying visit twenty years earlier, entirely suited this somewhat phoney palace. Shorn forever of its Baroque core and converted into an agro-sylvicultural gymnasium, the palace is a highly successful architectural trompe-l'oeil. The shell may be empty, but the exterior is amazing.

At the beginning of 1779, a great charlatan of a magician made his way onto these premises in order to be presented at the court of Duke Pierre de Biron. Courland at that time was seen as the promised land of occultism. The Great Cophta, as the magician was known, a follower of the Egyptian rite, opened a new Masonic lodge, "At the three crowned hearts", and astonished the Courland nobility with his tricks. It was said that he made the dead appear in mirrors. His visit caused a sensation, giving rise to heated argument among the cultured elite after his departure. Some considered Giuseppe Balsamo to be a hoaxer and a lunatic, an enemy of the Enlightenment; others saw him as a great healer, his high mind accompanied by a divine spirit.

Fifteen years earlier, another far more acceptable rogue, Giacomo Casanova, had been presented to Ernst-Johann de Biron. The old duke was immediately smitten. In his *Memoirs*, Casanova relates that the conversation came round to the mineral resources of the grand duchy and that he went so far as to "trot out anything that his enthusiasm had put into [his] mind". Attracted by these remarks, the Duke of Courland begged Casanova to inspect the mines he owned. The latter, easily persuaded, roamed the length and breadth of Courland for a fortnight. When his mission was completed, Casanova reported back to the duke, who was very satisfied, and who enquired whether as recompense Casanova would prefer a jewel or money. "Prince, I told him, from a wise man such as Your Highness, I make bold to accept money, since this may be more useful to me than jewels." Everything we find delightful about Casanova is here: a man both audacious and resourceful, receptive and cheerful, and totally uninhibited.

Our young companion knocks on a door and introduces us to a man who offers to take us to see the crypt where the dukes of Courland are buried. It is situated in the cellars of the palace, not far from the university canteen. He makes a great show of creating the right atmosphere, walking on tiptoe and lowering his voice, but the spectacle leaves me unimpressed. The crypt is a pleasant-enough display of lugubriousness, very neat and tidy, but rather tedious too. It smells like a 1960s cinema: a stench of old velvet and musk. There are the coffins. Reading the names still inspires daydreams: Jacob Kettler, Ernst-Johann de Biron and his wife Benigna, the grandparents of the Duchess of Dino. But the "perfect moment", which ought to come into play in such circumstances, is not in evidence.

This sudden confluence of awareness and objects is something Joëlle and I both joke about and invoke. It all depends on this sequence: revelation, the minute of penetration, the perfect moment. I experienced this state of total communion just once in Courland, at Sabile, at the top of the "wine hill". It is a sort of ecstatic shock that often wells up like an urgent message after gestating for a long while. It is not contagious, alas. Up until now, I've been the only one of us to experience it. A quizzical glance can ruin it.

Before leaving us, the young man points out a tree in the palace gardens, planted, he maintains, on the occasion of the marriage of Louis XVIII. Given that Louis was already married to Marie-Joséphine of Savoy – he neglected her a great deal, it is true – I imagine that our young friend is referring to the marriage of the Duc d'Angoulême to Madame Royale, which occurred on 10 June, 1799. Having been sent back to Austria in exchange for French prisoners, and after a long

173

period in Vienna, Marie-Antoinette's daughter eventually agreed to travel to Mitau to marry her cousin.

I have read several accounts of the wedding, none of which mention the planting of a tree, but that proves nothing. Marie-Thérèse of France, of whom we have a gloomy, sullen image – scarcely surprising considering the horrors she had endured at the Temple – was still, at this time, a beautiful twenty-year-old woman, well proportioned, with an agreeable, if slightly sad, face. The man to whom she was engaged, on the other hand, was not well endowed. A freak, it was said, with an inane expression but as honest as the day is long. It is likely that the marriage was never consummated: the Duc d'Angoulême was impotent.

For a tree planted two centuries ago, the one we've been shown does not seem very impressive. The bark has a purplish-grey tone. The dark, shiny leaves are slightly serrated, a different colour on the underside – grey verging on yellow – and a bit downy. I pick a leaf and tuck it into my notebook. At least I have not come to Mitau for nothing. I know that I am taking away a memento of a rather pitiful event: the marriage engineered by Louis XVIII was a travesty. Childless himself (he, too, was impotent), the king had dreamed up this union between the orphan of the Temple – the focus of a cult in émigré circles – and the insignificant Duc d'Angoulême, who played the role of dauphin. A pathetic farce: Louis XVIII could have been in little doubt regarding his nephew's ability to ensure his family's continuity.

This is not the story that I have assigned to my notebook. The leaf means nothing, but I have picked it. I cherish the illusion that the ceremony of 10 June, 1799, binding the fate of two survivors doubtless aware of the buffoonery behind the event, dwells in an eternal present. This leaf is imprinted with the strange reality of Mitau, a stone palace plundered by history.

Traces remain, apparently, of the chapel in which the marriage was celebrated. But, as far as the guide is concerned, I have displayed too little interest, and he is no longer prepared to make the effort. The visit is over.

A significant detail: the marriage of Madame Royale and her cousin was blessed by the Abbé Edgeworth, the Irish-born priest who attended Louis XVI in his final moments, shortly before he went to the scaffold. I am not superstitious, but the newlyweds certainly left nothing to chance. Edgeworth, who died in 1807 at Mitau from typhus caught from French soldiers wounded at Eylau,* whom he had looked after with the help of the Duchesse d'Angoulême, is supposed to have been the author of the famous words uttered at the very moment that the guillotine was about to fall: "Son of St Louis, ascend to heaven" – a probably apocryphal remark which our history books have repeated ad infinitum.

Mitau. A visit that nevertheless ends with an historical allusion: this palace built by an Italian whose life remains a mystery. Where did Rastrelli learn his trade? Who were his teachers? He sprang from no-one knows where, already forty, and began the building of Rundale, the Birons' summer residence.

Courland, the reverse image of Italy? One of my hypotheses when we first set out. Simplistic, obviously. The affinity is not clear, but it is there. "Reverse" as in "reverse shot", that is to say "facing", the original meaning of the word. Courland, the converse image of Italy? The blind spot or interface of Europe, a protected place, a territory the visitor wants to make into a sanctuary at all costs? A land of dreams like the one Stendhal invented for himself?

We stand at the side of the road, surrounded by traffic, gazing at the eviscerated palace. The other Europe is there, facing us.

175

IV

THE HOUSE ON THE LAKE

I was a Courlander
I watched, I drew breath
And I became a ship.

KNUTS SKUJENIEKS

WINTER

"Do you think we're going to be stuck here until the end of winter?" Joëlle says, not without a touch of anxiety in her voice. I have been assured that the traffic keeps moving in spite of winters which, at this latitude, can sometimes be harsh. The roads are quickly cleared of snow. Furthermore, for some years now climate change has apparently made the Baltic states unrecognizable. The cold is far less intense, snow increasingly rare. This early arrival of winter does not augur well.

Snow forms contours around every shape. As night falls, the soft whiteness takes on a pearly tinge, then an iron-grey colour. Wooden steps lead down to the lake. Because it is frozen, one could easily reach the far bank. There is not a single building on the horizon. Silence and whiteness reign. The dark mass of pine trees and the bare outlines of beeches and oaks interrupt the landscape's monotonous beauty. The wind causes the snow to flutter over the frozen lake in a fine white powder. When we slide open the bay windows, a gust of polar air blows violently through the sitting room like a silent explosion, causing condensation. The swishing noise made by the windows being opened also brings with it a muffled sound from outside, a simultaneous rumbling and hissing made not by the wind but by a deeper voice. We scarcely ever hear it in our latitudes; it is a wild, brooding sound that humans have not managed to tame entirely. I have noticed this strange noise made by the wind only once before, on the Kerguelen Islands.

Prisoners of winter, we are marooned in an isolated house. In the midst of snowbound forests, the place does not feature on any map. The only person nearby is our landlord, who lives 200 metres away.

This house, which harmonizes with the scenery, is a godsend. Blending with the lake, it provides perfect continuity between inside and outside. I have never lived in such a transparent place: light-coloured wood, pale shades that make the rooms seem bigger, a variety of lighting sources. The whiteness of the snow extends throughout the rooms. This could be unpleasant given that it is freezing outdoors. Quite the reverse; we feel as if we are at a show, enjoying an exceptional relationship with nature that allows us to see everything outside. Inspired by the Finnish architect Alvar Aalto, this ultra-modern creation, which can justifiably claim to be a new way of living, disappoints in only one detail: the minute size of the kitchen. The delicate aroma of new wood and the embrocation characteristic of saunas fill the air.

We decide to go into Talsi to do some shopping. From the house, you have to travel along a seven-kilometre snowy track through great expanses of forest in order to reach a road. Dwellings are few; several farms along the track have been abandoned. At the junction, a *kolkhoz* lies in ruins. The walls are that awful brick, somewhere between beige and pale grey, an apparently indestructible material from the Soviet era. The road signs have a secret significance. At the entrance to the town, a mysterious signpost reads *Apvedecels*: the name of a village, perhaps. This haunting word symbolizes Courland's enigmatic quality.

Talsi is a reasonably attractive spot boasting a large lake just below the town (it is frozen over at the moment), a mansion that has been converted into a museum and some old wooden houses in what might be called the historic centre. Snow banks, their tops blackened by a superficial thaw, are piled here and there along the high street. To say that the town's appearance, in these latter days of November, is tinged with exhilaration would probably be an exaggeration, but the exoticism of the place precludes any tendency to melancholy. We are a long way from Paris, from French alacrity and that Gallic blend of scorn and febrility, that hyper-irritation you sense everywhere that is actually indifference to other people, to what is happening, to situations. A fundamentally *inattentive* pose, which the sociologist Erving Goffman describes as a "polite imperviousness". Here, there is no electricity in the air; passers-by look a stranger in the face, without provocation, but they do not linger. Everything is solid. There is no fluidity in the street or in the way people walk past one another. There is no place for the changeable and the elusive among these people, who only seem to be comfortable with what is real and authentic.

We make our acquaintance with the supermarket. It differs from ours in France only in the extraordinary range of beers and vodkas. The wine shelf is very limited. Nevertheless, I spot a Spanish Rioja, a cabernet sauvignon from Chile and a South African merlot, all at very reasonable prices. France is represented by a few clarets and burgundies from wine merchants famous, alas, for their mediocrity. I find a *telogreika*, literally a "body warmer", one of those fleece-lined military jackets from the Soviet era that keep you incredibly warm. They were much sought after on the Russian front by shivering Wehrmacht soldiers, who pulled them off prisoners or corpses.

This supermarket is a delight. The girl at the butcher's counter, who sports a vaguely satanic punk look, speaks good English and takes pleasure in describing in detail the sorts of meat she is selling. The queue behind me shows no sign of impatience. I feel a bit embarrassed. I may be abusing my status as an "alien"; I should like the girl to be more succinct, but she continues to list the merits of each and every cut. The line of shoppers listens quietly. I observe their calm faces. These comfortably dressed young women – their well-cut coats are not devoid of elegance – look somewhat severe, but in tiny details – the way they blink, or toss back a lock of hair, or draw imperceptibly closer so that they can hear better – it is obvious that they are all eyes and ears. They don't want to miss a thing, even though it is vital that they should not be seen to be listening. They have not been taught to smile in public. Any sign of friendliness or kindliness on first contact can be misinterpreted as a charm offensive, even a seduction. It doesn't mean to say that there is not a lot of brooding going on, inside.

In one of the aisles, I come across a tall blonde woman of a certain age, still good-looking. She stares at me, then looks round after we have passed one another. I tell myself that she could be Mara. Would I be able to recognize her, in fact? I'm not sure I would. I cannot even remember the colour of her eyes. The stranger's eyes were brown, or seemed to be. I am bothered by what I assume to have been an unexpected encounter. I pace the aisles several times. The apparition has vanished.

"Look, that's your Canadian girlfriend!" Whenever, in town or village, we come across a woman of about fifty, preferably quite attractive, I bear the brunt of this jibe from Joëlle. She says "Canadian", not "Courland". Perhaps it's a way of trivializing the old story.

We have decided to prolong our stay. "The truth of this land is the winter," the Professor said. I, who do not much care for snow, equating it with emptiness, depression and the hollowness of death, have had to make myself do this. There is no reason to hurry: Henri has scheduled my article for the spring. This protraction, which he has assumed is another of my crazy ideas, no longer concerns him. I have negotiated the purchase of the Skoda Favorit that I rented this summer – a very good deal.

THE RESURRECTOR IS A PAINTER

It happened at Edole, in midsummer. I was at last on the trail of the Resurrector, who was conducting excavations in the grounds of this nineteenth-century building built on a medieval hilltop.

I had been wandering round the park, which is situated below the house, pacing by the lakes for a long time. However much I searched among the irises and syringas, there was no sound of digging, no human presence. The park had been taken over by birds making one hell of a racket. Their songs rang out eerily over the countryside. During the early days of August, the weather had changed, bringing the first chill of autumn. I feared that yet again I had missed the man for whom I was searching. Then, walking towards the entrance to the house, I noticed someone lying on his stomach on the grass. His head was bent over a sheet of paper, probably a map. He appeared to be writing. There could be no doubt: it was he.

The man was preoccupied. He had not heard me coming. As I drew nearer, I could make out what he was holding. It was not a pencil but a paintbrush.

"Good morning. I didn't know you painted."

"I do paint, actually. But, you know, it's not that unusual."

He spoke French. I had finally got hold of the Resurrector! He was not as I had pictured him; I had imagined an older man. With an expression at once lively, thoughtful and slightly inquisitive, furrowed eyebrows and a triangular head narrowing to a square chin, he did not resemble the vagrant figure of death and resurrection I had seen in my mind's eye. To tell the truth, I had imagined more of a landowning type, someone stockier, probably less sophisticated.

"I thought you were working in the park."

"The park is very beautiful, especially the lake with its lilies, but I'm mainly interested in relics, in ruins."

"Yes, you look for traces. It's your job."

"In a sense you're right. Beautiful things are in a state of suspended animation; they have a tendency to fade. I resuscitate them in my own way."

"I don't see how else you could do it."

Curious: I had the impression that the man I was speaking to was somewhere else. Why was he talking to me about "beautiful things in a state of suspended animation"? Exhuming missing persons is a noble task, but there is nothing aesthetic about it.

"Are you the Resurrector?"

"My name is Laurent de Commines. I'm a painter."

The misunderstanding had the effect of cheering him up. I was appalled. He seemed delighted: "I felt that something was not quite right."

He was fascinated by the history of the Baltic barons. For him, too, it had all begun with the word *Courland*: "The word had such a pleasing sound, and its reverberations have always stayed in my mind. I kept visualizing a wintry land full of snow-covered forests and well-stocked lakes, out of which strange castles emerged as if drawn by Gustave Doré. In them lived melancholy monarchs who spent their nights hunting stags or studying the stars."

He burst out laughing. I can see him now, meticulously arranging four little jars in his box of watercolours. "Oh! I know: these are fairy-

185

tale images. I'm still stuck in my childhood – I hope to stay this way for a long time." He had visited almost all of Courland's grand houses. He did not paint them, he reinvented them, drawing inspiration from caprices, those pictorial variations of free and unexpected forms that result in unusual compositions.

He took some samples of his work out of an album. He may have admired Piranesi, Pannini, Emilio Terry and Josep Maria Sert, but his style was like no-one else's. These were strange stage designs depicted in a surrealistic nocturnal setting. Beginning with the architecture of a specific house, he would compose dreamlike designs, reproducing motifs from vases, jewellery, statues and ancient monuments.

I recognized the manor house at Blankenfeld. He had used it as a feature in a setting composed of playing cards and chess pieces. Equally astonishing was the manor of Kratovicé, which no longer exists. De Commines had recreated it with the plot of *Coup de grâce* in mind, providing the house with an air of destruction and pillaging. You could see bayonets and an Iron Cross, a staircase turned upside down, a pitted ceiling. I reckon that in his own way he had depicted the disaster foreseen by Keyserling.

He told me about his first trip to Courland and the shock that he, a Westerner from a temperate country, had experienced. To begin with, I did not understand what he meant.

"The Northern European flora emitted a strange sense of expectation. I beheld a countryside exulting in greenery and light, but something in the rustling of the trees, the roughness of their bark and the massive bulk of their trunks suggested an underlying restlessness. The Courland summer is short. I was already feeling anxious about winter, that long, frozen, nocturnal silence. The cosmic sense of the northern forests has left a deep impression and made me understand the aspect of German and Baltic sensibilities that is both emotional and cerebral."

This was a revelation. In his remarks I discovered something of the excitement that had been at the root of my own journey. This man was an accomplice. I felt as though I was in league with him even if I did not share his melancholy view of the past. He did not realize that he had just opened up a new perspective for me. The brevity of the summer, the sudden lurch into winter ... Thanks to him, my visit was taking on another dimension. I was not immediately aware of it. I teased him by treating him as a decadent. He accepted the epithet with gratitude: "I have invented a world for myself. I glamorize it. I know, of course, that it's not real. I live inside this bubble. I only emerge in order to preserve this delicate film laden with dreams so that it doesn't get destroyed."

I sensed in de Commines a profoundly dejected attitude towards a modern world devoid of grandeur and the love of beauty. He had turned his back on it in that attitude of defiance we associate with the dandy, but he was managing to survive fairly well, remaining impervious and finding refuge in the illusions and fantasies of the past. I liked his pride, his conceit in presenting Latvians with a history they did not wish to see.

"The Romans and the Neapolitans were unaware of the value of the ruins of Antiquity. It took artists from elsewhere to make them appreciate their riches, their evocative power. With all their craving for modernity and Western comfort, the Latvians don't realize the treasures this lost world holds. It's precisely because it is no longer real that this world has become a means of artistic expression for me."

As we were parting, I thought, de Commines is the real Resurrector. Was he not exhuming what had been squandered? Was he not rescuing what no longer existed from oblivion? He was not merely excavating ruins, he was bringing them back to life by reinventing new forms. For a while, I believed in this conjuring trick, which made up for my own disappointment. But the delusion did not last. This painter had certainly opened my eyes, but it was not he who would provide me with the information that my cousin required. Only the employee of the Volksbund Deutsche Kriegsgräberfürsorge had the power to do that.

It was after this encounter that I realized that I would never understand the real Courland unless I spent a winter there.

ENCOUNTER WITH THE RESURRECTOR

I was to encounter the Resurrector by chance a few weeks later, in Riga. The cultural department of the French Embassy had asked me to take part in a discussion entitled "Courland as a Source of Literary Inspiration". Probably because I am not at my best when debating, I am not keen on such events, but I had agreed to participate, reckoning that the exchange of views might prove useful. In the programme, my name had been transcribed phonetically, as is the custom in Latvia: *Žans Pols Kofmans*. Taking part in the debate in front of an audience of about fifty people was a young Latvian writer, Rimants Ziedonis. I liked him right away. Without overdoing it, he voiced his opinions about Courland in an unaffected manner and with much humour. He could not get over the fact that a Frenchman should be immersing himself in his country. But his astonishment was bogus; it was a subtle way of expressing his support for my venture. The writer in him obviously knew what could be extracted from such a place. He confessed to me that he himself had succumbed to the illusion of Courland.

I should mention that Rimants' father, Imants Ziedonis, is one of the best-known writers in the country, the great regenerator of Latvian poetry and prose. Before taking up literature, the younger Rimants had worked for several newspapers in Riga. He had been sent to Australia to investigate the Latvian diaspora. It was on this journey that he made the acquaintance of an unusual Courlander, Arvids Blumentals, also known as "Crocodile Dundee", a native of Dundaga who became famous through Peter Faiman's film. "Go to Dundaga, you'll understand everything," Rimants told the audience. I listened to him talking about Courland, which he had traversed from top to bottom. He emphasized the importance of the coastline, long out of bounds, which was beginning to yield its secrets: "Paradoxically, the cross-border conditions imposed by the Soviet army saved the coast from excessive development. There is not a single factory there, nor a sanatorium, nor a tourist centre. They cut the trees down purely for logs to keep the officers' wives warm."

The embassy's cultural section had had lengthy passages translated from Rimants' most recent book, *Paradoxical Latvia*; these were read out to the audience. If I understood correctly, in this work he had used Courland for satirical ends. He had imagined, for instance, the revival of the Livonians, Latvia's most ancient race, now on the point of extinction. This Finno-Ugrian people, who live in northern Courland, must number no more than 500. By employing a mirror effect, Rimants allowed the Latvians, with their racial survival also under threat, to see their reflection. Aware that she was in danger because of a worrying drop in the birth rate and the drain of her young population, Latvia was fiercely protective of her language, the one factor that gave her an identity.

Rimants opened unsuspected horizons for me by revealing the existence of a giant radio-telescope situated to the north of Ventspils. This long-secret installation played an important part in what he had to say. Nicknamed "the Soviets' big ears", the device enabled Moscow to listen to its adversaries' conversations. The aerial mast was 50 metres tall; the description of its scaling by a Livonian separatist amused the audience. He had tied a huge kite to it on which the following words could be read: "I'm smarter than you, bitch!" Although the word *bitch* does not have a particularly disparaging meaning in this country, for Rimants, it symbolized the Latvians. According to him, the same method of innuendo had been used by poets in the 1960s and '70s to mock Soviet power. Literature benefited from the constraints of that time because writers were obliged to resort to invention and metaphor. Latvia withdrew into art and intellectual speculation.

So what remains of the Russian occupation? "The mythical radiotelescope at Irbene is still there. These days it enables us to observe everything under the sun, even though we have known for a long time that there's nothing going on, that the lapwings are no longer building their nests there, and no-one is declaring war."

After the lecture, the meeting was opened to the floor. Several people asked my opinion of Courland. I mentioned the beauty of the name, its strange and poetic resonance. I realized that Latvians did not understand the magnetism the word aroused in French. A tall fellow stood up: "Courland, it's the land of the Cours, a seafaring race who lived in the western part of what is now Latvia. They were stubborn and brave, and eventually they were defeated by the Teutonic Knights. Why do you find them so entrancing?"

Most surprising of all was a man at the back of the hall: "I don't know whether the word *Courland* is enthralling, but its history undoubtedly is. The sad thing about Latvia is that it has a history of always being subjugated, whereas Courland was master of her own destiny for nearly 240 years. It's an undisputed fact: Courland will always be a world apart. Latvia's upheavals, any agitation that sweeps the country, always stems from Courland . . . Remember the 'Courland cauldron'! The ferment lasted until May 1945. In forty-five years the bubbling has calmed down; the surface has not been stirred. But I am sure it will start simmering again . . ."

The man sat down. Like a good half of the room, he was probably French, in spite of a slight accent I was unable to place. I did not have much time to observe his face, because some of the audience seemed to be disagreeing. There was a slight murmur of polite whispering. I imagined the commotion such provocative remarks would have caused among a French audience. "A history of always being subjugated" was not a pleasant phrase, and I'd have thought that Latvians have just as much pride as we do.

My opposite number, Rimants, was amused by the turn the debate was taking. I suspected him of fuelling the argument: "The gentleman is right: Courland is the cradle of Latvia. Our state is based on the Courland model." This assertion was vigorously contested by a middle-aged woman: "One should not attribute to Courland qualities she does not possess. The independence of Latvia, in 1918, was the expression of a people who were at last free to do what they wanted. We didn't need the example of Courland. All the same, this allusion goes back some time, to 1795 . . ."

The freewheeling conversation continued around the platform for a long time. One should never chatter on too much or be overly polite after a discussion. I would learn afterwards that the man who had made the unorthodox comments was none other than the Resurrector, who had been passing through Riga. Why did he not introduce himself after the meeting? He knew that I had been searching for him for a long time. What was most frustrating is that he had lingered for a while, waiting for the discussion to end. Seeing that I was continuing to chat, he must have given up and slipped away.

CROCODILE DUNDEE

A quiet day, cold and dry. The sky is a very pure, clear blue. The snow forms a glittering crust that crunches like salt beneath one's feet. Flakes drift over the lake like thistledown in spring. This feathery indecision in the icy air produces a sense of serenity, of sobriety almost: the lake is in harmony with the world, as if it epitomizes the cosmos. The unsettled, unpredictable weather that raged all of yesterday has gone.

Ideal weather in which to go out. For a few days now I have been trying in vain to get in touch with Elize S., a *Courlandaise* who teaches French literature. She has translated into Latvian a number of writers such as the Marquis de Sade, Jules Verne, Françoise Sagan, Samuel Beckett and Georges Simenon.

Our landlady confirms that the roads are safe, that all roads in Courland are good roads: "No-one is afraid of the winter here." She is wearing felt boots, those Russian *valenki*s that are so effective against the cold. I have noticed that she has a heightened sense of Courland identity. According to her, Courlanders are a tough lot. They are also hard to win over, apparently. The casual joke, or banter, is not to everyone's liking. She keeps her distance without being brusque, even with a certain sweetness, avoiding familiarity. She performs a thousand small tasks: laundry, sawing, woodworking, weaving – I sometimes hear the clatter of the rods on her loom. She is a taciturn woman, absorbed in her work and fully concentrated on getting it done. Once the end has been achieved, there is nothing left, certainly not words.

The roads and smooth tracks are actually easier to drive along than they are in summer; the snow has levelled out the bumps and potholes. Our Skoda is comfortable cruising along on the frozen cushion. I cannot pretend that these endless white spaces thrill my soul, but I have grown used to them. The dark mass of the forest is a distraction from the whiteness that levels out and simplifies each and every shape.

Up until 1955, groups resisting the Soviets – the Brothers of the Forest – took refuge in these woods. Supported by the locals, they were mercilessly tracked down by the occupying power, which managed to get rid of them either by turning them or by having them denounced. Mara's uncle, who vanished without trace in 1946, was a Brother of the Forest. It was his tragic fate that persuaded the family to leave Europe for the New World.

The emptiest and loneliest roads have unlikely bus stops. There is always somebody waiting. I am impressed by these people's stoicism. I never see anyone being picked up.

The names of the villages are Antini, Vitolini, Rubeni, Lutrini, Egli; it is almost as if we were in Italy.

Lunch at an inn by the side of the road where dozens of lorries registered in Estonia or Lithuania are parked. The smell of the oil-fuelled central heating permeates the food. Pea soup with bacon, stewed beef as tough as the sole of an ice skate. Fortunately, there are some delicious rye rolls flavoured with cumin. I don't think foreigners are able to fully understand our French obsession with the pleasures of eating. They compare it to a form of enjoyment which for them is tantamount to lust. How can one explain that this fondness is not lustful? It is a form of rejoicing, not just in a physical way but in an intellectual one, a search for meaning, for sociability, and it distresses us that it is not shared. When travelling, the French are not looking for sophis-

194

ticated cooking, but for food that is simply and carefully prepared. Cooking that is timed to perfection, and produce that tastes purely of itself, require not just training but also experience, and instincts that are virtually second nature. Forty-five years of Soviet rule have damaged the Latvian people's taste buds.

Dundaga, Dundee, Crocodile Dundee: I have taken the writer Rimants Ziedonis' advice. The opening scenes of Peter Faiman's Australian-made film, starring Paul Hogan, take place in this small town in northern Courland. Arvids Blumentals was born in Dundaga between the two wars. The Soviet occupation in 1945 drove him, as it did 200,000 other Latvians, to leave his country and settle in Australia. There he became "Harry the Crocodile", the best-known hunter of large reptiles in the land; he must have caught over ten thousand. When hunting crocodiles was made illegal, he went back to prospecting for gemstones, digging for opals and setting himself up with a mine which he converted into a tourist site. People came from all over to visit.

At the entrance to Dundaga is a concrete statue of a crocodile on a bed of stones. This monument, erected in 1995, is dedicated to the small town's hero. It is difficult to imagine that this man's adventurous life should have begun in such a place, but Ziedonis is right: it was the stillness, the melancholy, the bucolic simplicity that prompted Blumentals to conquer the great spaces of the Australian bush. He had no choice.

This is the paradox of Courland. It has the appearance of a dead-end place, a doomed land, but, if one looks more closely, this sense of containment – typified by Dundaga – serves to exhort people to audaciousness, to risky initiatives. Two factors conspire in this: the seductive sea and, even more importantly, its replica, the sky. Even though the horizon is broken up by the enduring forest, Courland conveys a sense of freedom and infinitude that have to do with the brightness of the atmosphere, enhanced by an endless supply of fresh air.

Even the solid mass of the castle, whose medieval aspect is visible from every vantage point, inspires risk and nerve, hallmarks of the Teutonic Knights who built the vast structure in 1249. This Germanic order had been founded in Acre, in the Holy Land. The eastward progress of its knights had to do with war and the crusading spirit, but also with "sport", as Sylvain Gougenheim points out: "Whatever harms the pagans, that is what makes us feel good."* Such was the mindset of these warriors who dreamed only of cavalry charges and creating havoc.

The castle walls are positioned on the exact axis of the summer and winter solstices, a sign that, in spite of intense evangelizing, the old pagan rituals had not disappeared. The man responsible for the Crusade of 1245 is depicted at the entrance: Dietrich de Grüningen, master of the order and conqueror of Courland. It was Dietrich who had the castle built. Helmeted and with his sword planted firmly between his legs, he eyes the visitor from his bas-relief. At his side, a man of God, Bishop Bertold, looks no more approachable. The eyes of these two characters are significant: the man of the Church peers towards the north, whence came the evangelized pagans, whereas the Teutonic figure looks towards the west, the land of his ancestors. Legend has it that hidden treasure lies at the point at which their gazes meet. So far, no-one has found it.

Repeatedly modified, the fortress fell into the hands of the Osten-Sackens, one of the best-known families in Courland, whose estate extended over 7,000 hectares.† One Osten-Sacken, who played an important part in the battles of Leipzig and Montmirail against Napoleon, was appointed governor-general of Paris by the coalition forces in 1814.

*

How would one fill the castle's rooms and endless galleries today? A few are used as concert halls or for wedding feasts. The place smells of cold corridors, disused chimneys and a hint of ammonia. In a dark corner of the ground floor is a well-hidden hairdressing salon. Three young women are waiting for customers. One of them, made up to the nines, is leafing through a magazine, while the second is doing her nails; the third is daydreaming in front of a mirror. It is all so unexpected that I ask Joëlle, "Don't you want to have a go?" She replies that she doesn't want to risk it: "You try it. You're the one who needs a haircut."

I walk into the room, past the three dumbfounded women – there is the same silence as when Clint Eastwood walks into a saloon bar, but I don't possess his nonchalance. I believe I've alarmed the three women, who remain rooted to the spot, regarding me with surly expressions. No-one smiles.

To smile spontaneously is considered the height of artifice and hypocrisy. Smiling should have meaning, and there is something preposterous about our presence here, but I only have to make a scissors gesture above my head for the women to start giggling. The overly made-up blonde seems not to be in accord with her colleagues. It's not clear why. Perhaps they only do women's hair? But it's not as if the salon is busy.

Eventually I am invited to sit down. The shampoo girl soaks my collar as she rinses my hair. I can feel the water dripping unpleasantly down my back, but this is a superior form of head massage! Her fingers gently knead my scalp: it feels divine. It is the manageress, apparently, who will undertake the most delicate task: my cut. I try to make her understand that she should not take too much off, that I need my hair to protect me from the cold. "Okay, okay, good," she says.

Silence falls over the scent-filled salon, a slightly unrefined combination of rice powder and violets. The aromas remind me of my childhood. All that can be heard is the monotonous sound of the scissors and the light swish of the broom with which the blonde girl is sweeping up the hair clippings. In the mirrors, I can see Joëlle leafing through a magazine. Suddenly I hear her say, "She's taking too much off! Stop! Stop!"

My hair has certainly been thinned! One cannot say that the girl has shaved my head, but she has well and truly shorn me. It's not a disaster, but it's not a great success either. My hairdresser seems disappointed by my lack of enthusiasm. I try to make her feel better. It is my fault: she interpreted my hurried gesture, made with the flat of my hand, as an invitation to cut my hair as short as possible, whereas I meant to indicate the reverse. When I come to pay, I give her the customary tip. The manageress looks amazed. Overcome by such generosity, she grabs a small, pear-shaped rubber flask. I choke under repeated blasts of the lotion she sprays all over my face.

Anyone can follow my trail now: I leave an overpowering smell of jasmine in my wake.

THE SURVIVOR

After my disappointment in Riga, I had been able to gather some information about the Resurrector, thanks to the translation of an article in a Latvian newspaper. To judge by the villages in Courland that he had been exploring, our paths had crossed several times during the summer. The article mentioned that his investigative work was based on Wehrmacht records, local sources and the testimonies of local inhabitants.

The only means of identifying a grave was by taking samples from between 20 and 50 centimetres below ground level with the aid of a mechanical digger. The article described the curiosity of the local people, who could sometimes be hostile if they were dealing with Russian-speakers. The Resurrector related that in the region of Aizpute, for instance, he and his driver were welcomed with the cry "The fascists are coming!" The excavator of tombs acknowledged that for those Latvians who lived through the immediate post-war years, digging up the ground meant digging up their past: "It is as if, after the Soviet interlude, they were going back in the wrong direction along time's one-way street. All of a sudden, they found themselves immersed in 1945. It is an experience that can sometimes be traumatizing."

He was not content simply to dig up soldiers' remains; he also tried to identify them. Money, jewellery, private papers and any other belongings he unearthed were sent to Germany. On several corpses he found a St Odile medallion, demonstrating that they came from Alsace.

By the end of his long campaign, which lasted between eight and nine months with a gap in the early winter, the Resurrector had formed a view about the war in Courland: "One cannot imagine the ferocity of the fighting. The final months were devastating: the constant gunfire, the noise, the cold . . ." To date, he and his assistant had discovered the remains of 25,000 soldiers. The article pointed out that many of their remains were being gathered in a large cemetery near Saldus. Feeling less than hopeful, I decided to make my way to the necropolis.

Each of the tombs is surmounted with a German cross carved in stone. A paved path free of snow leads to a further tall cross overlooking the burial ground: 14,000 Wehrmacht soldiers whose bodies were scattered throughout Courland are interred here. Panels inside a recently constructed brick building relate the ossuary's history.

For ten minutes or so, a solitary individual has been wandering around the small exhibition room. He eyes us suspiciously, then turns away to examine the numerous German pennants and standards draped on the walls. Finally, unable to control his curiosity, he comes over and asks whether we are German.

"No, French." He smiles. "Ah! I see, you're Alsatians," which is partly true. He thinks we are searching for traces of a parent who fought on the Courland front, which is not entirely wrong, even though we are here somewhat by accident.

The man says nothing more, regarding me in a sorrowful, slightly detached way. He is wearing a Tyrolean hat and a thick, perfectly cut grey overcoat. I find his manner odd. He never stops punching one gloved hand with his other fist. This sound, at once muffled and abrupt, makes me uncomfortable. To shake off my malaise, I consult the register listing the soldiers buried in the cemetery. The list is long, taking up several volumes. The names mean nothing to me. But each of the birth dates, followed by the death year (mainly 1944 but also 1945), is of interest. The majority perished before reaching their twentieth year. Meanwhile that pounding noise of leather on leather reminds me of a boxer working away at his punchball. Perhaps the man has something he wants to say to us?

Above the registers are messages stuck to the wall. They are all in German, apart from one: "I am looking for my father. Elisabeth G., wife of V." The address and phone number correspond to those of my cousin. I think I recognize her handwriting, yet I am positive she never came here. This discovery, which ought to astonish me, nearly makes sense. If you think about it, this new cemetery, which will be by far the largest in Courland, is the ideal place to obtain such information. My cousin probably entrusted this note to some *malgré-nous* of her acquaintance who made the pilgrimage to Saldus, or to the relative of another soldier. I am aware of my cousin's inventiveness and obstinacy, but I'm annoyed that she never said anything to me about this.

The documents in the exhibition reveal a devastating vision of the 1945 battles, images of endurance and terror as all was collapsing: trenches covered in snow, tanks paralysed by blizzards, men chilled to the bone. Under normal circumstances, troops stationed in Courland would have been sent home to Germany; under siege, the Reich needed all its available men. But Hitler did not want these units to be moved, wishing to use them to counter-attack the Russians on their flank. In February 1945, just as the Red Army was nearing Berlin, he rejected an evacuation plan. The same request would be turned down bluntly when Admiral Dönitz suggested a disciplined retreat.

Up until the Armistice of 8 May, 1945, the armies in Courland would have received regular supplies by convoy and submarine. Throughout the war, the Soviet Baltic fleet was unable to leave the Gulf of Finland, the only exit by sea being blocked. The Germans called the Baltic the "*Binnenmeer*", the "inner sea". For them it was a German lake.

Snow is beginning to fall. I gaze out of the window at the spectacle. Millions of snowflakes are being blown horizontally against the pane like rubber balls which break into a myriad of needles, only to liquefy three or four seconds later. Not all the particles burst on the transparent surface; some bounce and return to attack the glass like insects drawn by the light.

The man with the gloves comes over. His high forehead appears anxious, his mouth is slightly contemptuous, and his prominent cheekbones grow taut as he looks me up and down. How old is he? Seventy at the most. You sense that he takes care of himself, that he is anxious about his physical well-being. In spite of his haughty demeanour, I sense that he is troubled. Clearing his throat, he says that, for him, this is a deeply moving place. He feels the need to confide in someone. Later, he tells us that he is a widower and that his children did not want to accompany him to Latvia.

He has just recognized the names of some friends on the crosses: "It's the first time I've been back to Courland since 1945. In 1941 I enlisted in the 126th Infantry Division. The fighting was terrible; it never stopped. There were six battles of Courland. The most terrifying of them took place in December 1944, right here, around Saldus. Miraculously, on Christmas Eve it all stopped. Total silence for two days. The fighting began again with renewed violence on 26 December. It was the noise that was the most frightening. That Soviet artillery fire, with Stalin's *katyusha*s, was a nightmare. I'm an amateur violinist. In my frozen hole, I held terror at bay by listening to the rising and falling tones of the gunfire. Eventually, I discovered a certain harmony in it.

202

The artillery was so close . . . The whistling of the multi-barrelled guns, the hissing of the shells before they exploded, the blasts and the reverberations were like a [here he used a German word to described a musical instrument, I think it was a sistrum]. To be honest, there's nothing to which you can compare a Soviet rolling barrage. A hellish music, but a music nevertheless, with its own crazy rhythm."

He spoke Franco-German gobbledegook punctuated with English words that were easy enough to understand due to his lugubrious diction. Though I transcribed his remarks, I can't vouch for them; although the words were clear, his explanations were disjointed. He frequently stopped to take a breath, as if gazing into a vacuum. I would never have imagined him to be a musician, but I found his method of taking his mind off his fear by translating bursts of gunfire into a melody emanating from a diabolical instrument infinitely moving. He admitted, however, that he often found it hard to concentrate: "The Reds rarely respected the rules of harmonic progression." He probably said "the Reds" the same way he did when fighting for the Wehrmacht. He spoke of them with a degree of respect, apparently because of their scant regard for danger, but he cursed them for leaving his comrades to die in the Siberian camps after the war.

Seriously wounded by shrapnel near Liepaja, the man owed his survival to this injury, which, on 8 May, 1945, caused him to be given priority to board one of the thirty-five Junker 52s that flew in from Norway. In a last-chance manoeuvre, these planes had succeeded in landing on a runway in Courland. Attacked on their return by Russian fighters, only three aircraft, of which his was one, arrived safely. "I'm a survivor. I ought to thank heaven, but I'm not fully present any more. Ever since those terrible days, I haven't belonged to this world. I'm an old man. I live like a hermit in Munich, but I'm not alone. I never left

203

my comrades. They're not just with me in my dreams; I chat to them every day. The cemetery isn't full yet. I'll be joining them soon."

The bitter wind moaning beneath the door is making the small room feel increasingly cold. I shiver. "Yes," he says almost regretfully, "we'd better leave. I like the cold. I prefer it to the mud. It does a lot of damage to an army. We suffered from the cold, it's true, but we were grateful when it arrived. It hardened the trench walls and the roads; it brought some order back into all that chaos. I could have come here in summer, but I preferred to come now. It reminds me of those terrible days." The words "terrible days", which he has used twice, have the effect the *Dies irae* has on me. The old man will never be able to blot out those days of wrath.

We wish him luck as we say goodbye. He does not quite understand the expression, which he takes literally: "A journey such as this has nothing to do with success or failure." As he closes the door of the red-brick building behind him, I have the sense of having locked him in there with his ghosts. I try to imagine his return to Munich. What will he have gained from this pilgrimage? Some peace? A final numbing of the soul? Increased disillusionment? I am not a great believer in the value of sentimental journeys, of opening the revenant's eyes to what he did not, or did not wish to, know.

This man's tragedy is not to have hidden the truth from himself but to know it only too well.

"IT'S A GERMAN NAME"

The Skoda almost got stuck in the muddy lane five or six kilometres from the lakeside house. A peasant who emerged out of nowhere managed to haul us out with the help of a cable attached to an M.T.Z. tractor dating from the Soviet era. My profuse gratitude was greeted with almost hurtful indifference. The moment the car was out of the mud, our saviour turned round and climbed back onto his tractor without even a wave. In its medieval sense, the French adjective *roide*, meaning "rigid", would apply rather well to this sort of behaviour. I must beware of generalizations, of course, but I have had enough experience of this lack of spontaneity and rejection of foreigners to think that they are fairly commonplace here. We are no more courteous in France, perhaps even more contemptuous, but at least our arrogance is expressive.

Elize S. is waiting for us at the restaurant. A hint of an accent, a pleasant voice, a mildly mocking inflection: she has mastered our language perfectly. A spry fifty-year-old with a face both intelligent and resolute, her impartial expression softened by a slight smile and an amused air. Nonetheless, she seems to be on her guard.

Elize S. is used to the French. She knows how to introduce the right note of light-hearted banter concerning our journey to the restaurant. She has learnt that it is customary for French people to explain the route they took in the utmost detail, information that is not at all interesting but which is intended to create a congenial atmosphere. Elize

S. puts up with the convention, though not very cheerfully. The waiter speaks a little English. (I haven't met a single one who spoke French. I think of that hero of Keyserling's who, lying on a beach in Courland, reads Fénelon in the original.* In aristocratic families they usually spoke French during meals so that the servants would not understand.)

Elize S. admits that interest in our language is on the wane in Latvia, though she is struggling to make it more popular with her students. *Struggling* may not be the best word with which to characterize her; she is clearly a fighter but, to my mind, one of the beguiling sort. She has a way of insinuating, of suggesting: "It's great to speak French, but my students say, 'What's the point?' English is the most common second language in Latvia, with French in fourth place. What's the point? The Soviet era didn't end in an instant: we remain ensnared by practicalities. You don't get rid of dialectical materialism just like that . . ."

She must know what she's talking about. I make a quick calculation: at the time of independence, she would probably have completed her studies and already have been teaching for some time. Her generation was immersed in Marxism for the masses: "We were taught about the 'self-awareness of the present', material conditions, the productivity of labour, the law of value . . . The younger generation just interprets *Das Kapital* however it pleases."

The restaurant is decent. The smoked fish is tasty and served on huge plates, an expression of culinary modernity. White table linen, a geometric arrangement of assorted bread rolls in a basket, discreet cutlery: Northern minimalism prevails naturally over the deployment of space and furniture. Not a sign of stew or of that insipid fried food that ruined the first half of our journey.

"We're getting ready to join the European Union." There is a degree of irony in Elize S.'s soft drawl. "Joining Europe is obviously a privilege. But perhaps you have too great a tendency to think you're doing us a favour. Before 1991, we belonged to another union, the Union of Soviet Socialist Republics. We were glad to withdraw from it. Having done so, now we have to prepare ourselves to join yet another one."

I don't think she could care less. She gives the impression of knowing how to prioritize life's difficulties. Entrenched in impassive aloofness, oscillating between reticence and imperceptible mockery, she is not the type to moan about the harshness or transience of our times.

We discuss Latvian patronymics. The most common ones allude to trees: Berzins (birch), Klavins (maple), Liepins (lime). I mention Mara's family name in passing: "It's a Latvianized German word. There are many of them in Courland." Elize S. gives me a curious look: "Do you know someone by that name? It's typical of the region of Cape Kolka."

She always speaks slowly, *recto tono*, careful not to make any mistakes. She says that with our language one has to engage with a logic that is not always coherent: "In your way of speaking, you can describe something in advance and then name it and develop it later. In Latvian, it's impossible to refer to something that will only be said afterwards. For us, the important thing in a sentence is the key word. Words that are quite natural in French, such as *exist* and *existence*, are only used in their philosophical senses in scholarly Latvian. I'm suspicious when French appears to be simple. Sagan, for instance, what a drag! Very difficult to convey! She seems so easy, but this apparent ordinariness is lethal, because she requires not just explanations but adjuncts too; otherwise one misinterprets her." Since she is talking about literature, I take the opportunity to ask her about the Marquis de Sade, whom she has translated. "Oh! Sade is horrible!" I ask her to explain. She sighs: "Those series of dependent clauses, those relative pronouns, those relative clauses . . . Sade is perplexing." I am not quite sure what it is that she finds so horrible about the author of *Justine ou les malheurs de la vertu.*

Elize S. says she adores France, which she knows well: "It's so bawdy! 'Very attractive, very French, tra-la-la!' That's how we see you French people. These stereotypes owe a lot to the Russians, who are still rooted in the clichés of the belle époque and mad Parisian life. Here, everything is drab and sad. The long winter nights . . . But we are an active people, different from the Russians, who just watch the river flow by in front of their houses. The demarcation line is us, the Baltic countries, the outpost of Europe. Beyond is the Orient, flux, laissez-faire, existential fog."

We returned to the lakeside house when it was dark, having got lost as we were driving into Talsi. The puzzling road sign *Apvedecels*, pointing to an unlikely village, led us further astray. In the menacing darkness, the word reminded me of the letters of fire at Belshazzar's feast: *Mene, Tekel, Upharsin*, especially *Tekel* ("You have been weighed on the scales, and you have been found to be wanting"). The country-side was deserted and oppressive. The shortness of the winter days confines people indoors and condemns them to long hibernation. Hence this remorseless twilight state, a sort of black wall along which one stumbles for seven or eight months.

A sense of solitude, an almost frightening perception of the dark and that yellow-tinged whiteness reflected by the headlights when the car has entered a forest, the realm of the divinities of the night. The slightest detail – a tree stump, a clearing, a pile of wood lit up in the snow, a tree trunk lying on its side by a ditch – takes on a disturb-ing aspect. The headlights cast a net into the night to capture evil monsters. There is nothing reassuring about the noise of the heating fan that breaks the silence; its monotonous sound is supposed to be calming, but the ventilated air only adds to one's anxiety. Hearing is night's overriding sense. The car seems to be forcing its way through a tunnel of cotton wool. It is not snowing, but hundreds of silvery specks are blown onto the windscreen.

It is a relief when we open the door of our dacha and the light bursts forth in the sitting room.

MYTHOLOGICAL COURLAND

Like dynamite, winter causes everything to disintegrate. The milder spells of weather reveal the ravages perpetrated by the cold. Its explosive power causes the roads to come apart, the dirt tracks to break up and the grass to char. It tears up, cleaves open, flattens out, eviscerates. Our lane is literally pulped: its core has been removed. It is nothing more than a succession of cracks and mounds. The rough, sodden, fragmented surface makes one think of breadcrumbs.

A visit to the Talsi supermarket. The same abundance as in France, and the same variety. But the people have not yet acquired the mechanical body language of the affluent. Do the young women who were barely emerging from adolescence when Communism came to an end remember the poverty that was rife at that time? I have the impression that they spend carefully. In any case, the customers do not appear to have reached saturation point. There is still something innocent about them. The breaking-in process is not yet complete. These shoppers are at the apprentice stage of consumerism. Not yet devious enough to be true Europeans: too sincere, too rigorous, too upright. There is a lack of theatricality, something to do with nature and the gods that remains primitive.

Perhaps that is what the "transition" is: a state of suspension, a power cut. The machinery is ready. The action that will put everything into motion is about to take place. The shoppers calmly making their way among the shelves are in a no-man's-land, a halfway place, a country in a hollow. Behind them, a utopia in ruins; ahead of them, a society of plenty that is just as uncertain, a model they will not give up at any price. Their turn has come. In the beginning, these shelving units and display stands assuaged their needs. Now they are hesitant, trapped between the indispensable and the desirable. One day, once they have yielded to it, the desirable will cease to excite them. They will then discover the melancholy of satisfaction, the refined weariness of the overdeveloped, the pride of doubt, the brazen certainty of beauty and truth.

Courland wavers between the old order, which has withdrawn, and the new one, which beckons. The people believe that the stakes are obvious: a choice between the weight of the past and the buoyancy of the future. In the theme park of Europe, what will be the place of Courland, child (along with others) of two European catastrophes? What will it excel at?

At the butcher's counter, the Goth recognizes me and turns her attention away from the customers waiting in a queue. Her main purpose is to show how well she speaks English, which is far from well. Like me, she uses English baby-talk, the flimsy lingua franca that enables one to be understood in all parts of the globe except of course in English-speaking countries, where slang, rapidity of speech and grammatical subtleties soon become discriminatory. (According to Elize S., one Latvian in seven speaks English.)

At the fresh-produce counter, I spot a Napoléon Camembert made in Poland.

At the checkout, a tall blonde woman is packing her shopping into a bag. I only see her from behind. She turns round: I feel sure that she is the stranger I glimpsed a month ago in this very supermarket. She gazes at me coldly for five or six seconds. I watch her disappear into the parking area. It is not so much that she resembles Mara – thirty years on, I find it hard to picture her – but the way this woman moves and especially her facial expressions seem familiar. It is as if an inner guide wants to give me an occasional clue but never tells me whether I am on the right path.

On the return journey we don't see a soul. Courland is the land of joyful desolation. These forests, these grand houses, these meadows constitute a particular kind of space. It is like spending a holiday in a state of expectation, laden with promises and pitfalls. Even if the space is not yet occupied, it is infused with a hopefulness which, no doubt, will be fulfilled, but at what price?

The rare accounts in French of travels in Courland all describe its peacefulness as if of another age. The most recent, dating from 1937, describes "a gentle land dedicated since the beginning of the world to Virgilian peace".* This was the vision, a century and a half earlier, of Madame Vigée-Lebrun: "In the woods, I saw Diana followed by her retinue; in the meadows, the dances of shepherds and shepherdesses such as I had seen on bas-reliefs in Rome." This vision of a mythological Courland, like a replica of Arcadia, a land of peace and happiness, seems straight out of a painting by Poussin. "I charmed my way,"† writes Madame Vigée-Lebrun prettily. Her "charming" of it hints at the pliability of this country, which allowed the imagination to fashion it as it pleased.

The notion of a joyful Courland has haunted other travellers, as a young German scholar, Anne Sommerlat,‡ has shown. In the Enlightenment, particularly during the reign of Pierre de Biron, Courland took on the sense of a "stylized elsewhere". In the manner of Voltaire's *Candide*, German writers employed it as "a geographical support . . . to transpose concerns of a political nature".

212

The depiction of a country with borders situated between the two worlds "of civilization and barbarism", fulfilling the function of a "cultural, political or economic bridge", reoccurs frequently in the writings of the eighteenth century. Sommerlat emphasizes the duchy's distinctive position, which manifested itself as an "historical anomaly". At the end of the nineteenth century, she explains, this uniqueness would transform itself into literary myth through Eduard von Keyserling's novels, which describe a decaying aristocracy powerless to break the shackles of a tradition that eventually stifle it.

Sommerlat could have extended her illustration into the twentieth century with Marguerite Yourcenar. The literary myth is all the more remarkable since the author of *Coup de grâce* never set foot in Courland. Yourcenar explained the reasons for her decision to Matthieu Galey: a besieged country mansion was the ideal setting for a love story involving three young people marooned in an atmosphere of war: "I felt there was a tragic beauty there, as well as a unity of place, time and danger, as our classics used to put it so marvellously."*

Yourcenar always liked to comment on her own books in retrospect, in order, no doubt, that critics and readers should not misinterpret her intentions. Published in 1939, the revised French edition of *Coup de grâce* was improved by a 1971 preface in which she highlighted the importance of her documentary research, which obliged her "to unfold the official maps, to gather up the details provided by other eye-witnesses, to search through old illustrated newspapers to try to find the slightest echo or the slightest reflection of obscure military manoeuvres on the frontier of a godforsaken hole". Where Courland is concerned, no-one escapes the term "godforsaken hole". Nevertheless, the regionalism in *Coup de grâce* remains fairly conventional: "Birch woods, lakes, fields of beetroot, squalid little towns, shabby villages", not to mention "Jewish usurers torn between wanting to make their fortunes and the fear of being bayonetted".

The note of authenticity is in the name of Yourcenar's mansion: Kratovicé, which has a vaguely Latvian ring to it. When Yourcenar was writing her book, all German names had been Latvianized. If she consulted maps, as she said she did, Kratovicé must have struck her as a plausible name, although the final "é" is never used in Latvian. Just as in the classical tragedy she invoked – she quotes the preface from Racine's *Bajazet* – no-one could care less about the setting. But in her preface, Youcenar curiously made claims for the accuracy of her notes by attaching importance to the testimony of people who had been involved in the war, as if to say, "I wasn't actually there, but look, I've got it right."

No doubt, this is one of the little affectations of someone who enjoyed putting her instinct for divination to good use, even where local colour was concerned.

THE CEMETERY

The horn of Kolka (Kolkarags). On a map of Courland, it is the first thing to catch the eye. This needle-shaped headland is the hallmark of the ancient duchy, the signature that guarantees its authenticity. What would Corsica, the *Île de Beauté*, be without tubular Cap Corse, other than an ordinary, shapeless expanse?

A few fishing villages – not that there are any boats or fishermen to be seen. Fifteen years or so ago, there would have been no point in coming here; the shoreline was infested with border guards pacing up and down the dunes with their dogs. The writer Rimants Ziedonis spoke of a coast beginning to reveal its secrets.

All I see are long beaches of white sand lined with pine trees that remind me of the coast of the Landes: the same iodized, balsamic scent, with a slight veil of mist that causes the waves to explode and smash into tiny droplets. In spite of the cold, a few people are having their photographs taken on the furthest point, a strange heap of rocks and broken bricks with the vague look of a demolition dump. It is worth the detour, nonetheless. To the east, the sea is perfectly calm; to the west, it is rough. "Swimming near Cape Kolka is dangerous" warns a notice. Cape Kolka is dreaded by yachtsmen who fear being wrecked on the long underwater reef. You can see how the sands carried by the coastal current are continually reshaping the tip of the headland as it becomes eroded, fills out again in a sort of perpetual motion, and eventually sharpens itself a little further out, only to become blunted again.

I continue to ignore the Baltic, unattracted by this surly, invariably ill-tempered sea, not bothering to inspect the endless beaches. However much I think about the "Mediterranean of the North" or the Hanseatic adventure, it fails to exert its charm. This not very inviting sea has an enclosed feeling. In fact, it is just that: there is only one exit, to the west, between Jutland and Sweden. Such containment makes it particularly vulnerable to pollution. Paralysed for so long because of the Cold War, denied its identity, it can now be perceived as a living form. Ever since the fall of the Berlin Wall, it has become once again a place of rediscovery and trade, accounting for 15 per cent of the world's commerce. On this wintry day, it is deserted.

The window of a grocer's shop at the southern end of Cape Kolka displays the shopkeeper's name. It is the same surname as that of Mara's family. This is the first time I have seen her name in public; this inscription gives it a physical presence. The grocer wears an apron; the young woman at the till is most likely his daughter. I search for a resemblance to Mara. The girl at the till is fresh-looking and rather pretty. About twenty, she has a welcoming appearance that is agreeably surprising. But with the best will in the world, she is nothing like my former lover. I can no longer recall Mara's features exactly, but her expression remains clear in my memory. I have one photograph of her, yet I don't remember throwing any away. They are lost, or rather, one day I forgot about them. Someone got rid of them. With his smooth manners, the grocer reminds me of Mara's father. I have a sudden desire to ask whether any members of his family migrated to Canada. But how to phrase the question? He probably does not speak English. According to Elize S., there are countless people in northern Courland with his surname.

The shoreline, frozen in an icy crust, resembles the frosted edges of a cocktail glass dusted in sugar. In a clearing we notice strange humps among the beeches and pines. These little mounds are fishing boats turned upside down. How was anyone able to haul them up to this undulating place far from the shore? Given their advanced state of decay, they must have been here for a long time. Some are no more than vague traces in the earth resembling piles of cinders. Time has dried and then gradually destroyed the hulls, whose frames resemble charred wood just before it is reduced to charcoal. Only the rivets are intact. A few bits, such as the rudders, the propeller shafts or the main masts, are still in place. These vessels, flat on their bellies, their guts exposed, look like fish taken out of the water and left to die. In the midst of the mangled boats, some trees have sprouted to a height of 8 or 10 metres. They make me think of stakes driven into the vertebrae of the hulls.

One is struck by the instantly tragic significance of the scene. The drama is tangible. You sense that these silent spots conceal a terrible event. In a bar, a few hours later, I learn the truth about the Mazirbe woods. After the Second World War, countless Latvians fleeing the Communist regime escaped to Sweden aboard fishing boats. In order to put a stop to this exodus, the Soviets ordered the Livonian fishermen to haul their boats onto dry land and drag them far from the shore into these woods, to render them unusable. I can imagine the despair of the Livonians, today Courland's only native minority: men of the sea deprived of their dearest asset, ruined, reduced to gazing at their boats as they perished in this clearing.

Mara had told me that her parents had fled Latvia, sailing from Courland to the island of Gotland, in Sweden.

I must see the boat cemetery again. The worn-out shells, about to be engulfed by the forest, have not passed into death. Resisting, they have not completely turned to dust. Their memories may be hanging by a thread, by a shape that will soon disappear. For years, people must have been forecasting their imminent disappearance, but the boats are still there, hovering between life and death; they are disintegrating, vanishing, but their imprints have not been obliterated.

Rimants Ziedonis mentioned the Livonians when we met in Riga. Like Finnish, Estonian and Hungarian, their language belongs to the Finno-Ugrian group. Spoken by a million people before the Second World War, it is now on the endangered list.* Ten years ago, there were about forty people who spoke it; today, there are no more than five. Livonian is destined to disappear because those five have not succeeded in passing the language on to their children.

Ziedonis had strongly advised me to visit Irbene, a few kilometres from Mazirbe. One of the Soviet army's secret bases, it was abandoned by the Russians in 1994. With a heavy heart, they were obliged to hand over to the Latvians their giant telescope, which was capable of picking up high-frequency radio waves in Scandinavia and the Baltic Sea. Christened *Zvezdotchka* (Little Star), the telescope is still, thanks to its dish measuring 32 metres in diameter, one of the most efficient in the world.

This enormous installation in the midst of the peaceful forest is like an apparition, an almost supernatural image that looms up as if in a science-fiction film. The huge reflector, perched on a pedestal as tall as the Arc de Triomphe, looks like a flying saucer about to take off. The site appears to be deserted. Grass grows between the concrete slabs; a pine sapling has even managed to take root in a crack. The site of a gun turret is filled with freezing water. The perimeter is enclosed with a barbed-wire fence whose posts are beginning to bend. The concrete walls are collapsing. A crumbling futurist universe in the style of Enki Bilal.†

Close to the telescope, hidden among the pines, is a small estate where the scientists, the military and their families were housed – approximately 2,000 people. The bare, crumbling buildings appear to be unoccupied. A man in his fifties springs out from behind a pile of snow. He sports a handlebar moustache. I wave to him. He does not respond. As he inspects me, he puts his cigarette to his lips, a movement that reveals a star-shaped tattoo on his wrist. Without saying a word, he walks over to the Skoda and stares at the registration plate for a long time. This little game is clearly intended to alarm me. In an unconscious gesture of defiance, I take out my notebook as if to jot something down. Unable to concentrate – my heart is in my boots – I scribble "radio-telescope" three or four times. Another man arrives, an equally sinister expression on his face. The two of them exchange a few words without looking at me. I may be mistaken, but, having acquired some familiarity with the Latvian language, its reed-like, metallic tone and that inevitable stressing of the first syllable, I think that the two guys are speaking something else, possibly Russian, easily recognizable by its brassy intonations.

"I think it would be wise to leave." Joëlle, who has witnessed the scene, takes me by the arm. We get back into the car. The two men make no hostile gestures. Perhaps I am imagining things. The disconcerting atmosphere of the place, the silence, the late hour, have probably heightened my awareness, inspired a wrong reading of the situation.

Later on, I learn that Irbene's radio-telescope had not been abandoned but had been converted into a radio-astronomy station specializing in the observation of the sun, and occasionally used for artistic experiments in the field of acoustics.

THE STRANGER

A visit to Talsi's museum, situated in the upper part of the town in the middle of a park with very tall trees. The collections are housed in a Neoclassical mansion that once belonged to a Germano-Baltic family, the von Fircks. The current exhibition is entitled *The Return of Frédéric Fiebig*. I am the only visitor. There are museums everywhere in this country, and in the most out-of-the-way places; even more astonishingly, they are always open. The receptionist is delighted to see a Frenchman, and to mark my arrival she sits down at the harmonium by the entrance and plays a waltz by Sibelius. The reason for her pleasure – not immediately apparent – soon becomes clear.

Frédéric Fiebig, born in Talsi in 1885, lived in Alsace, where he died in 1953. After studying in St Petersburg, he soon emigrated to France. A Post-Impressionist to begin with and later an Expressionist hailed by Apollinaire, Fiebig was the personification of the *poète maudit*. Between the wars, having retreated to the Vosges hills with his daughter, he painted bare, geometric mountainous landscapes verging on abstraction. In 1935 he settled in Sélestat, where his painting took much of its inspiration from the Alsatian countryside. Penniless and cantankerous, having sunk into oblivion, he died, totally abandoned, in a hospice for the poor. His work is much sought after today. Maurice Rheims, a member of the Académie Française, contributed to a monograph on Fiebig entitled *Des plaines de Courland* [*sic*] *au Ried alsacien*. Nowadays the artist is considered as one of the masters of

Alsatian painting. There is something implacable about his powerful canvases.

Fiebig leads me back to Alsace once again. Is this a coincidence? More than ever, I need to heed this inner call. Perhaps it will set me back on track on this disorderly Courland treasure hunt.

What is Fiebig doing here? Why did he leave Talsen – the town's name before the First World War? Fiebig, who was in all likelihood a Germano-Balt, had been born a Russian subject (like Mark Rothko, who came from Daugavpils). In Courland you are constantly juggling German and Latvian names, especially those of villages and grand houses.

As I leave the museum, I am surprised by the presence of numerous cars parked along the pavements. People in their Sunday best, carrying single flowers, are walking towards a building, probably a school. All are dressed to the nines; the women, heavily made up, leave a whiff of chypre perfume in their wake. On a podium, a man appears to be reading out a list of names, and the audience is applauding. In between the announcements, a singer intones a monotonous, melancholy tune resembling a *cantilena*. It reminds me of the *dainas* that Mara hummed for me, whispering, "You're wrong; they're not sad."

I position myself discreetly near the podium in order to observe the onlookers. I know of nothing more moving than the facial expressions of a crowd avidly watching the same spectacle. In this instance, all heads are turned towards the singer. The faces are different, but the expressions are identical, somewhere between gravity and emotion. What is most touching is not the features they have in common but their extraordinary concentration. They don't see me even though I am staring at them shamelessly.

Among the audience, one person intrigues me. The only woman whose eyes are not fixed on the platform, she gazes at me with a

221

worried expression. Could it be the stranger I glimpsed on two occasions at the supermarket in Talsi? Her appearance is both imposing and anxious. This proud and awkward quality reminds me of something, though Mara did not have that slightly hurt, disdainful look. Yet there are similarities in the harmony of the woman's features and that Grecian nose. And her expression? If there is one thing that changes very little in one's life, it is one's face, the way one moves one's head or frowns when examining something.

She is still observing me. The show is starting to become repetitive. Perhaps I am becoming bothered by her presence. What should I do? I am leaving Courland in a week's time. This journey must have had a purpose. Should I allow this opportunity to pass me by?

The show continues. Supposing the woman leaves before the end? She looks bored. There is something at once hard and beseeching about the manner in which she regards me. All of a sudden, I see her pushing through the crowd, extricating herself calmly without looking behind her. I follow her. We move away from the others. I walk over to her; her pace has slowed.

"Are you Mara?" She shakes her head in an irritated, almost unpleasant way. "Aren't you Mara?" She does not answer. I am convinced that it is she. Then she brusquely turns away and starts speaking in Latvian. Could she have forgotten her French?

"You . . . you used to speak French so well!"

Turning back to me angrily, she gesticulates as if to stop an insane person from speaking . . .

V

THE RETURN

Courland is far from being a contemptible land.

MIRABEAU

REVENGE

I don't know whether my journey had inspired me or not; in any case, writing the article did not require much effort. Is lack of application a good thing or a bad thing? The story was never published. Henri was going through difficulties at his magazine. Had he lost his touch? Had the financial people decided the joke had gone on long enough? A week after receiving my article, he rang to tell me that the magazine had ceased publication. He was appalled: "It's infuriating! I thought your work was remarkable." This time I was the one who had to raise his spirits.

Several indications, in fact, led me to think that he had not read my article, or that he had just skimmed it. I was not annoyed: he had other fish to fry. He tried to console me by suggesting that I offer my piece elsewhere. He had nothing against the idea, having arranged for me to be paid even though it had not been published. I have never tried to place the article elsewhere. Not out of any virtuous motive but because I could not be bothered. Perhaps, too, out of a sort of loyalty to Henri. The matter concerned only the two of us.

I might as well not have wasted my scruples. A few months later, while vaguely sorting through my archives – a grand word to describe a pile of notes, documents and articles dumped in cardboard boxes – I realized that I couldn't put my hands on the article. No copy existed apart from the one I'd sent to Henri, but he had vanished at the same time as the magazine. Data storage on computers was still in its infancy, and, in my case, light years away.

225

This loss did not upset me particularly. I'd think about it occasionally, but the journey itself mattered more to me than the telling of it. On reflection, however, my visit to Courland had all the appearances of a failure. I had not even fulfilled the mission with which my cousin had entrusted me. She claimed to have been very disappointed when I told her how the Resurrector had eluded me. For months, she had cold-shouldered me following this dereliction, an attitude I reckoned was unfair. Nevertheless, I had to admit that the interest of this Baltic trip had been partly to do with searching for her father's grave or for some indications that might enable one to identify it or discover the circumstances of his death. No doubt I had also set off to uncover another trail – but was it really a trail?

There had been nothing to uncover, unless it was Mara's shadow.

And the music of the word *Courlande*, which had so fired my imagination? I needed to find out whether the harmonious consonance of this name, which had a great deal to do with Mara, added up to anything. There again, I could not claim that my trip had been a success. At no time was I able to establish a connection between the country and Mara. I believed that I had glimpsed her on several occasions, however, and the appearance of the woman at that school in Talsi had made a strange, even a disturbing, impression on me.

That the balance sheet was inconclusive should have made me more indifferent. And this was what nearly happened, until one day a lanky young man with a blank expression and a nonchalant gait turned up at my house in the 14th arrondissement of Paris.

I did not recognize him straight away. He was wearing a tight-fitting military overcoat with gold buttons and black mock-leather trainers with a Batman logo. If I failed to identify him, it was because of the Armani sunglasses, which were probably fake. There was a deliberately spurious aura about this fellow, an ironic manner that was quite appealing.

It was Vladimir, the polytonal rocker from Karosta. I was all the more astonished to see him since I felt certain that I had not given him my address. Our parting had been fairly cool. He had asked me to send him an English–Latvian dictionary. I had promised that I would, and I did manage to do so a month or two after my return. I had of course written the sender's address on the package. I never knew whether he had received the volume, and in any case I did not expect him to acknowledge receipt or thank me. He was not that sort of person.

I have noticed this attitude among people from the former Soviet bloc: a total lack of inhibition compared to us in the affluent West. Now that the wall has come down, they no longer ask, they demand. They consider the objects they are requesting as their due. They regard us as the spoilt children of a consumer society whom it is normal to exploit.

This behaviour does not shock me; quite the reverse. In a cowardly fashion, without a second thought, we abandoned them to their oppressors. For forty-five years, we left them to their drabness, to their wretched poverty, making the most of the good times without concerning ourselves with them. Now they are in a position to make demands. They ask for their fair share even as they exploit us. I rather admire this lack of consideration on the part of these revenants from the dead. Yes, we felt sorry for them but always in a patronizing way. They were long-suffering, touching even, with their eternal plastic carrier bags, embarrassed by their ridiculous cheap clothes.

Vladimir's demand was not outrageous. I expect he must have been amazed when he received the dictionary. Among all the tourists whom he shamelessly solicited, here was one who kept his word. He must have thought that it would be worthwhile getting in touch again.

Over two years had passed since my trip to Courland. Vladimir felt no inhibitions about turning up at my home without warning. Having invited him to come in and take a seat in the drawing room, I immediately regretted doing so. He plonked himself down on the sofa in an unrestrained way that I could not help but admire, displaying his high-top trainers with their Velcro straps.

Unwisely, I offered him a whisky. He probably construed this as an inducement to stay where he was. I therefore had to listen to his adventures since he had left Karosta. No longer in sync with his polytonal rock band, he had decided to leave for Ireland, where he had become involved with a vaguely Goth community rock group. But he soon fell out with them: "I'm not very good at getting on with other people. I'm alone among my contemporaries." Alone among his contemporaries! What self-importance! As I listened to him, I reflected that he had still not solved his identity crisis. Rather than be a Russo-Latvian without any ties, one might as well go west and become a sort of stateless person.

After Ireland, he had lived in London, Amsterdam and then Berlin. He had been in Paris for six months. He was well aware that he had made a double defection, from both his blood (Russia) and his homeland (Latvia). "I am a transcendental traitor," he kept on saying. I don't know where he had picked up this pompous new vocabulary. It did not fit with the indifferent attitude that had struck me in the past. He was more relaxed than ever. Except with the whisky, of which he requested another glass, and then another, without appearing in the least drunk. He told me about his life in Karosta and the changes that had occurred in his country. In his wanderings across Europe, he had been inspired by an overwhelming desire to make up for lost time, to compensate for all the deprivations. Nowadays, he wondered what freedom he had acquired through contact with consumer society, other than the sense of a new type of dependency: "The lack of warmth in your countries is dead boring. I prefer the coldness of Courland."

My irritation gradually vanished. I even took a certain pleasure in hearing him talk about his deprived city. Karosta represented a memory at once dramatic and pleasant. I had liked those rickety buildings, those electric wires hanging like ivy from the balconies, the poverty and solidarity, and a gift for improvisation that made me not nostalgic – I detest that sort of sentiment – but happy. I was glad to have known Vladimir's country at such an uncertain moment: a people who were convalescing, who had still not recovered from the shock of regaining their freedom and who were at the same time anxious to progress quickly, to hasten their reunion with Europe.

Vladimir had wanted to progress quickly and see this paradise for himself. As might have been expected, he had been disappointed and felt let down. How could it have been otherwise? "The world I've seen offers no more surprises. I've been there." (What pomposity!) I pointed out that he had only seen a tiny part of this world; he should not draw hasty conclusions. "You're right, Monsieur. I look at France, and I fail to understand you. However, there's one thing you're better at, and that's loving your own neuroses." He explained that he admired our pretensions and our love of danger, our way of moving forward, as if this conduct had its own logic and justification. A kind of behaviour that was always being debated: "You like the strain but not the collapse." His comment was not inaccurate, even if it was rather simplistic. We French are so vain that we even love criticism, so long as it isn't directed at anyone or anything in particular. Vladimir was probably just indulging my self-esteem.

After six months in France, my polytonal rocker spoke French fairly fluently. As I surmised, he had learnt it from a French girl with whom

229

he was apparently in love. This allusion was the only time when I sensed that he had changed and was both vulnerable and anxious. Who knows? This liking for conflict and his misunderstanding of our people, as well as his reluctance to adopt radical solutions, probably had something to do with his own situation. Joëlle had arrived home. She didn't recognize him immediately. She could not take her eyes off his black trainers with Batman stamped on them.

Like me, my wife had superlative memories of Courland. We had visited a number of countries together, but that one could be compared to no other. The trip had been a strange interlude. Far from being of secondary significance, it had been an unusual digression in so far as it had taken us out of our normal pattern of existence. We had travelled in many more exotic and unfamiliar countries. Why should Courland – a part of Europe after all, with its familiar grand houses, forests, landscapes and behaviours – evade all attempts at description or definition? It was impossible to relate our impressions to any other reality that we knew. How to explain why we had adapted so well to Courland's emptiness, had even become strangely acclimatized? A sense of time standing still, of suspension, of a complete break. We had truly been "on holiday".

Taken up with other projects, I had put Courland to one side, and then, all of a sudden, this rocker had turned up from another planet. His appearance gave substance to our memories. Before he left, he gave me his latest disc, recorded in Berlin. He was turning to breakcore, a style of music that blended techno, rap, funk and rock. On the cover of the C.D. was a reproduction of a vaguely familiar painting: three weeping nudes draped in black and standing in front of a catafalque, one of them displaying her bottom. It was a painting by Clovis Trouille, *Mes funérailles*, very much in the style of this erotomaniac, anarchist artist, hailed in his time by the Surrealists; the musical *Oh! Calcutta*, which took its title from a painting of his depicting a pair of buttocks, had made him famous in the 1970s. The back of the C.D. cover featured Vladimir, dressed like a rebel chieftain from the Colombian jungle, wearing a plastic bath hat and flippers.

I don't know much about rock music. After he left, I immediately listened to Vladimir's C.D. He had said that it was an attempt at "metallurgical rock". I had thought of heavy metal, of groups like Deep Purple or Rainbow. He had objected: "No, no, it's something else."

It began with a din like the noise of a hydraulic drill, or a mill wheel, or a grinder, with all sorts of computerized sound effects. Then, a voice both mellow and husky, which quickly became angry and frightening: the voice of Vladimir. These fragments produced a mixture of roughness and sweetness, for, after the wild surges, the song became soft and tender. The harshness of the guitars briefly gave way to the lightness of a violin, and then the ghastly metallic racket started up again, before being gradually becalmed by less piercing, more melodic notes above which rose Vladimir's warm, pleading voice.

It was not a C.D. I would have listened to all day long, but for a philistine like me, this music possessed a morbid and incantatory power reminiscent, with a bit of effort, of a painting by Trouille. Some people regard him as a minor artist, because his compositions resemble colour prints, but their iconoclastic and derisive qualities have universal value.

There was a strange number called "Kurland Beef", the only song sung in Latvian. According to the cover blurb, the words had been inspired by a *daina*, that Latvian quatrain with the poetic concision of the Japanese haiku. The song was about a "motley-coloured cow" stuffed with coke, as well as about Mara, the Great Goddess.

Mara. I could have taken this reference to my Courland-Canadian lover as a wink from Fate, particularly since she had once sung these poems to me, but Mara is a fairly common first name in Latvia. In that country, which converted to Christianity fairly late, a type of animism is always is evidence. Mara represents destiny and femininity. Vladimir was invoking both the goddess and the motley-coloured cow, using a play on words that obviously escaped me. Later, I discovered that the goddess Mara is also associated with death.

I saw Vladimir again on two occasions. He had asked to read the article I had written about Courland. When I told him what had happened, he said, "You can't just leave it there! You've got to get your own back, Monsieur. You must write a book." I laughed. Write a book when I could not even recall what was in the article I had written for Henri!

Such amnesia was significant. All I remembered was that I had written a well-considered piece, colourful and reasonably enticing, full of historical information, with a few facts and figures about the economic situation. It was certainly not the worst piece I had ever written, nor was it among the most exceptional. It was exactly the type of resumé that Henri liked: a few factual bits, a cheerful tone and, above all, not conceptual – he loathed anything conceptual, a term that for him was synonymous with "obscure". As I had told the Professor before we took leave of one another at Ventspils, I had not mentioned anything of genuine interest.

Apvedecels, for example: that disturbing word I had mistaken for a warning sign in the countryside, and which had repeatedly caused me to lose my way. Probably because I had pronounced it incorrectly, nobody had been able to tell me what it meant until Vladimir told me it meant "diversion". This revelation summed up my Courland adventure rather well. I had never experienced such a frustrating journey. In the end, I had bungled everything, and Vladimir turning up in my life merely highlighted my disappointment.

What had I seen of the inhabitants, of their lives? Not much. The language difficulty had a lot to do with it. In *L'Italie en 1818*, Stendhal describes travellers who were only interested in old stones and buildings and who took no notice of how life was being lived: "All they saw were walls." Had what I had seen in Courland not merely been the illusory power of walls?

During the months following Vladimir's visit, I started to reread Keyserling's novels. And, most importantly, I came across a book I had not known about at the time of my trip: *The Outlaws*, an autobiographical novel by Ernst von Salomon, who had fought with the *Freikorps* in Silesia and the Baltic states after the defeat of 1918. The fate of this young cadet who had been trained in the harsh Prussian education system intrigued me; it immersed me once more in the area's troubled history. Von Salomon had been part of the risky enterprise known as the *"Baltikum"*, which attempted to bring all the territories formerly occupied by the Teutonic Knights under German control. A bleak book, profoundly nihilistic and obsessed with death, *The Outlaws* is steeped in an end-of-the-world atmosphere; I have seldom read such a despairing and brutal book. Part of the plot takes place in Courland. Von Salomon clearly was captivated by what he calls a "curious country"; he wrote of a "saturated land" that seemed to "suck him in". I, too, had experienced that absorbing power.

In 1919 von Salomon was convinced that a decisive struggle was being played out on these fringes of Europe: "We were searching for the entrance to the world." The entrance to the world! A striking image with which to describe Courland, the last floodgate between the Germanic and Slav entities. His story emphasizes the difficulties involved in gaining access to this intermediary space, which is unrivalled in its capacity to hold up and repel the invader. What is most incredible is that this *Drang nach Osten* (thrust towards the East) nearly succeeded, thanks to a remarkable piece of strategy on the part of General Rüdiger von der Goltz, who was officially responsible for defending the borders of east Prussia against a Bolshevik invasion. Having landed at Libau (Liepaja) in February 1919, the commander-in-chief of the northern *Oberkommando* army found himself confronted with four enemies: the Bolsheviks, Latvian government troops, the Libau military council and the Allies, the victors in the war, whose fleet was guarding the Courland coast. "Following good old strategic principles", he wrote, "I decided not to fight them all at once, but one after another – starting with the Bolsheviks."

Born in 1902, Ernst von Salomon belonged to the *Freikorps* which crushed the Spartacist rebellion in Berlin and then set off to Courland as volunteers. Dangled in front of them was the prospect of acquiring land at the end of the campaign. Von Salomon rejoined both the Baltic *Landeswehr*, made up of members of the Courland aristocracy who were of German extraction, and Colonel Bischoff's Iron Brigade, which would become the 10,000-strong Iron Division.

Under the command of von der Goltz, the German troops routed the Bolsheviks and made their entry into Mitau, a spectacle which von Salomon described with ruthless cruelty. Before they fled, the Reds massacred hundreds of prisoners, rounding them up in prison court-yards and hurling streams of grenades at the tightly packed groups: "Other hostages were tied to the horses of the Red Army cavalry and whipped with knouts as they were dragged from Mitau to Riga."

It was in these circumstances that von Salomon came across the necropolis of the dukes of Courland, which had been desecrated by the Communist troops. The army rabble had hauled the corpses out of their tombs, propped them up against the walls and "pumped them full of bullets". A few days later, von der Goltz took control of Riga. In the course of the fighting, one of the leaders of the Baltic *Landeswehr*, Hans von Manteuffel, who was looked upon as a hero by his soldiers, was killed. Manteuffel! Yet another familiar name, linked to that mansion at Kazdanga that I had visited not long ago, just before making the acquaintance of the Professor.

The Outlaws made an impression on me not just because of Courland but also because of the tragic vision of the world emanating from it, which foreshadowed the disasters of the twentieth century: the fascination with violence, the hatred of democracy, the cult of the charismatic hero, the decreasing instinct for conservation and transcendence, the death wish, the will to power.

"What we wanted, we did not know, and what we knew, we did not want." A decent description of the adventurer, the man in a headlong rush.* Von Salomon's account manifests a degree of admiration for the Baltic barons "intent on saving their age-old traditions, their strong and sophisticated culture, at all costs" – a vision radically different from that of Keyserling, the observer of a society that was no doubt highly civilized but was clearly on its last legs.

Von Salomon would later be involved in the murder of Rathenau, the Minister for Foreign Affairs, escaping the death penalty because he was under the age of criminal responsibility when it occurred. I wanted to know more about him. This militant nationalist was just the type to join the Nazi Party, as a number of his colleagues did in 1933. Curiously, he kept his own counsel, criticizing the lack of culture and the demagogy of the National Socialist leaders. This did not prevent him from being sent to an American internment camp, since the Allies suspected him of having supported the regime, an experience he described in *The Questionnaire* – the title refers to the 131 questions

235

every German citizen had to answer in order to gauge their degree of complicity with Hitler's regime. These writers' names and these connections were like clues in a treasure hunt.

I immersed myself happily in this free entertainment.

A LETTER

One day, in a garage in the 14th arrondissement, I made the acquaintance of a car salesman. He had given me his card: Nicolas de Osten-Sacken. Osten-Sacken, the name of the family of Baltic barons whose mansion I had visited: Dundaga, the birthplace of Crocodile Dundee. I wanted to know more. We agreed to meet.

A quiet young man of about thirty, with a meticulous way of speaking and a friendly manner, Osten-Sacken received me in his office. I thought he had lost all trace of his origins, but he knew the name of Dundaga, where his family was from. He himself had never set foot in Courland: "'*Noblesse oblige*', our father used to say when I was a child. I was steeped in worship of the past. My father spent his time doing research. He would tell us such stories that I sometime wondered whether he was not making them up. Going to Courland is not a priority for me. I'm saving it. I've just had a son. Every human being is the descendant of a long line, noteworthy or not. One day I'll tell him where he comes from, and perhaps we'll make the trip together."

He persisted in speaking of his family as a "Russian branch". I corrected him, explaining that the Osten-Sackens had only become Russian when Catherine II had annexed the grand duchy in 1795: "You are a Courlander." He probably could not have cared less, but his good manners concealed this.

With his well-cut striped suit, his somewhat cool politeness and his modesty, Osten-Sacken hardly corresponded to one's notion of a car

237

salesman. "I love this job. I was a lowly police officer for six years. Night duty and apprehending criminals! I was idealistic. I believed in protecting widows and orphans. I became disillusioned. Here I'm happy."

In his working life, he called himself Nicolas d'Osten: "It's easier to remember. It sounds like Nicolas de Staël." The name Osten-Sacken appeared in full, however, on his visiting card. I had brought with me a Latvian book of photographs of Courland's palaces and manor houses. He recognized Dundaga, in particular the engraving of a hunting scene in the romantic style, with, in the background, the former outline of the feudal fortress: "This picture is part of my childhood memories. My father had it enlarged and coloured like a painting." We leafed through the book together. He identified his family's coat of arms, and was able to explain the emblems and colours. The arms of the owner were reproduced next to each of the houses. He was astonished to see them alongside other residences besides Dundaga: "I didn't know all that belonged to my family." He told me that the only thing his grandfather had been able to bring out of Courland was a sabre, which his father had sold to an antiques dealer. All Nicolas d'Osten knew about his great-grandfather, also Nicolas, who had died in 1948, was that he had fled his country in 1919, via Turkey and Germany. After spending time in France, he had decided to settle in Tangiers, then an international zone.

A customer came into the garage. D'Osten walked over to him with an attentive air. I waited for a few moments, at which point he came back, saying, "Please forgive me. My job ..." Before we parted, he observed, "We are what we do, not who we're descended from." A fine turn of phrase. I believe it was the first time he used it: he searched for the right words and hesitated before using them (unless he was simply a good actor). He disappeared for a few moments to photocopy the pages from the book illustrated with houses that had belonged to his family.

This encounter aroused my curiosity. What had become of the Germano-Baltic families after the disaster? A number of them had sought refuge in Germany – the descendants of this diaspora still publish a magazine, *Nachrichtenblatt der baltischen Ritterschaften*. Some of them had settled in France.

The most extraordinary adventure was that of Théodore de Medem, a descendant of the most illustrious family in Courland – Anne-Dorothea, the mother of the Duchess of Dino, who married Pierre de Biron, was a Medem. When Latvia regained its independence in 1991, Théodore de Biron returned to the land of his ancestors to try to regain possession of his family's former properties (more than ten houses and 55,000 hectares of land). His plan was to renovate these residences with the help of European funding and convert them into luxury hotels. He tried every avenue and even met the President of the Republic, Mrs Freiberga, but – apart from a few people who were directly involved with the country's historical and cultural heritage, such as Imants Lancmanis, the curator of Rundale – the Latvian authorities made no effort to support him.

Nationalized in 1920 by the Republic of Latvia, the former possessions of the Courland nobility are today inalienable. In certain cases, the state can concede these properties, but in Théodore de Medem's opinion the conditions are "draconian". Nevertheless, in 1995, he, along with his wife, had the satisfaction of being granted Latvian nationality, probably the only Germano-Baltic noble to be treated in this way. After many trials and tribulations, he returned to France: "To our great regret, we do not think we shall return to Courland. It's a wonderful country, but they have failed to turn over a new leaf. Our families have paid a heavy price for the country's chaotic history. Fifty years of Communism and the Latvians' hatred of the Germano-Balts have left their mark. The Latvians don't want to acknowledge their past. For them, the history of their country began in 1920, which is tantamount to excluding eight hundred years of a fascinating story."

Today, Théodore de Medem lives in Panama. With his wife, he has opened a furnishing and interior-decoration shop with the aim of spreading and promoting French *savoir-faire*.

I chanced to meet my former colleague Dorothée at a dinner party. She had not changed. My recalling her grandmother and Courland aroused no more interest than they had when she was at *Le Matin de Paris*. Evidently, she had no wish to revive "these stories about ancestry" that had blighted her childhood and youth. During the course of the evening, I droned on about her forebear Dorothea, Duchess of Dino and wife of Talleyrand's nephew, who combined beauty and intelligence. To no avail. The account of my travels in Courland, on the other hand, intrigued her. We saw each other again. I gave her a book, *Les Trois Grâces de Courlande*, written by an American.*

The first of these "graces" was the mother, Anna-Dorothea von Medem, Grand-Duchess of Courland; the other two were her daughters Dorothea, Duchess of Dino, and Wilhelmina, Duchess of Sagan. The mother was nicknamed the "Venus of Courland" or "the divine Anna". The mistress and confidante of Talleyrand, she was considered one of the most influential women in Europe. As for Wilhelmina, another beauty, she was the great love of Metternich, who trusted her judgement completely. According to her contemporaries, the Duchess of Dino, the last of Talleyrand's loves, surpassed her mother and sister because of a matchless charm that men found beguiling. Dorothée loved the book about "the Three Graces". She, too, began to succumb to the captivating power of the Circe of Courland.

Though not at the forefront of my mind, my interest in Courland resurfaced, ironically enough, through reading, meetings, even disappointments. I returned to Canada on several occasions. For a long time I did not bother to find out what had happened to Mara. Some of my friends there had known her well. It was only after my trip to Courland, during a stay in Montreal, that I felt the need to ask after her. To no avail: they had all lost touch.

One day I went to Outremont, recognizing without difficulty the street and the number of the house where her parents had lived. The place had not changed except for the fir tree by the entrance, which had become enormous. I rang the bell; a woman's suspicious voice asked who I was. I gave a few confused explanations. To my great surprise, the door opened and a charming young blonde woman appeared, a baby in her arms. She knew of the house's former occupants, who had sold it in the early 1980s; she did not know what had become of them. As she was speaking, I recognized the hallway and thought I caught a vague whiff of candles, a feature of the Mara years.

In January 2001 I received, via my publisher, the following letter:

22 January 2001

Dear Jean-Paul
I don't know whether you remember me, Mara from Canada, your Maja desnuda. *I confess that it would never have occurred to me to write to you had I not come across a book of yours,* The Dark Room at Longwood, *I think it is by you, and not by someone of the same name. The book is rather reminiscent of the young Frenchman I knew in the late 1960s. I was very touched that you began the*

book with the first sentence from La Chartreuse de Parme: "Le 15 mai 1976, le general Bonaparte fit son entrée dans Milan à la tête de cette jeune armée qui venait de passer le pont de Lodi, et d'apprendre au monde qu'après tant de siècles César et Alexandre avaient un successeur."*

Perhaps you remember my admiration for Stendhal. You used to tell me that the beauty of this sentence stems from the adjective "jeune", which gave it a particular cadence and sharpness. I liked your book and I will not squabble with you (squabble is a French word you taught me) over the fact that you were being disloyal to your king Louis XVIII. Do you remember? You were grateful to him for having brought us together.

All that is a long time ago, but one can't forget the self-confidence of those youthful years. I think that if I was taken with you at the time, it was because you were disconcerting and you made me laugh a lot. I'm not sure about the word disconcerting, for, alas, I have less and less time to practise my French. It touched me that you took me for a naïve young thing. You were a puritanical libertine. I liked this mixture. You irritated me sometimes by taking me for a Nordic or Scandinavian person. The Baltic people suffer a great deal from this inability of the outside world to know who we are. In Canada, I felt I was a Courlander, but now that I live in Courland, I don't see any Courlanders. I realize that the inhabitants have lost their identity. They'll find it again one day, I feel sure.

From my first marriage, I have a boy and a girl. I married again, to an American from Detroit of Latvian origin. After independence, we decided to settle in Latvia. I live in a small town in the centre of Courland. I shall soon be a grandmother. My two

children stayed in Canada, and, once or twice a year, I go back
to Montreal to see them. I also wanted to let you know that my
parents died before 1991. It was sad for them: they never saw their
country free again.
With love,
Mara

I would not say that the letter surprised me very much. To tell the truth, I had been expecting it for thirty or forty years. She had simply taken her time. When I thought about it, my self-esteem took a blow, however. These lines probably did have emotional undertones but only in so far as they applied to Mara's youthfulness. "The self-confidence of those youthful years": what did she mean by that? A sort of casualness or innocence perhaps. And the term *disconcerting*? Not very flattering. Why not "odd"? "My king Louis XVIII"? I had never had any affection for this monarch, merely a soft spot for his having enabled me to get to know Mara. I recognized, however, that history has been unjust to this sovereign who ultimately understood his age better than Napoleon did. The latter lost his sense of reality after his marriage to Marie-Louise; he was mistaken about himself and about the French people at the time of the *Cent-Jours*.*

"Puritanical libertine": not a bad thing to have been at the time. When I think about it today, Mara was far more liberated than I was, with that Latvian pagan quality that I had observed on my trip. I liked the slightly old-fashioned word *taken*, not much used nowadays, and which she probably remembered from her French reading. One sentence bothered me a great deal: "It touched me that you took me for a naïve young thing." Another word probably dug out of Stendhal or Balzac: the revelation that she thought of me as gullible rankled, even

243

forty years on. It seemed that she no longer practised our language very much, since she had read my book in an English translation.

The letter also informed me that she was about to be a grand-mother. This disclosure troubled me deeply, as if Mara had not been endowed with a youthfulness the years could not touch. Who knew! She may even have become plump, ugly, slovenly! The tone of her letter, however, suggested that this was not the case. She took care of herself. The choice of words, whose meaning she must have weighed carefully, suggested a certain smartness, including that hint of coldness she had adopted at the beginning of our relationship. It was significant that she gave no address. She provided a few bits of information about her life, but she did not want to rekindle our past, an attitude that I completely understood but which opened yet another wound and affected me deeply. I no longer interested her; her memory of me was not powerful enough to contemplate rapprochement.

Another thing disturbed me: the knowledge that, on my journey, it may well have been she whom I had encountered. She referred to a small town in the centre of Courland. It could have been Talsi.

I showed the letter to Joëlle. Clearly, the allusion to "puritanical libertine" amused her greatly. She sympathized slightly, though not without a degree of irony, as if to say, "You've told me quite enough about this business! So is that all it was about?" She may well have been right. Had I not been fantasizing all those years or, at the very least, embellishing my relationship with Mara? Had I not allowed pipe dreams to replace reality? Mara gave the impression of having lived through this youthful idyll without it affecting her particularly. I had passed through her life like some kind of exotic actor, vaguely symbolizing the figure of a Frenchman such as might have appeared in the books she was reading.

Such revelations could have dealt a fatal blow to my wavering infatuation with Courland. Quite the reverse. Vladimir was right: I had to have my revenge. There was something unfinished, unfulfilled, about the story. My indecision had lasted for too long. I would write a book. Not immediately; I had other tasks to complete. But the decision was made: I would return to Courland. This time, I would prepare myself. Not as on the first trip, when I had left too much to chance. I had been very lucky to meet people like the Professor.

The Professor had been disappointed to hear that my article would not be published, but he did not let his disappointment show – I was only too aware that deep down he must think of me as a shirker. Was this why he delayed visiting me in France? We had never lost touch. In one of his letters, he wrote of his joy at having driven the Skoda Favorit, as if it were some mythical car. He had been sorry to hear that we had broken down a few kilometres before arriving in Riga. He wanted to know why this had happened. I did not know – we had rushed to catch our plane. The exchange of New Year's greetings allowed us to take stock of our respective lives. This was how he came to inform me about his divorce, without telling me, however, that he had a new partner. I heard a few years later of his remarriage to one of his students, twenty years younger than him.

His first trip to France was memorable. He came on his own and wanted to see everything. I took him to Bordeaux, where he was made welcome at a few friendly chateaux. He had boned up thoroughly on the subject and had made noticeable progress as far as wine-tasting was concerned. What touched me the most was that he had read the entire works of Eduard von Keyserling. He continued to consider Ernst Jünger as a joker, however.

I did not know the date of my journey yet, but I was going to devote the months prior to my departure to getting myself into shape. One day, during this period of preparation, I rediscovered my notebook. The leaf that I had picked in the park at Mitau fell out from between the pages. The souvenir of the marriage of the Duc d'Angoulême and Madame Royale . . .

I had completely forgotten about that story. I immediately wanted to discover the name of the tree. I showed the leaf to a friend who was keen on botany. *Sorbus intermedia*, he reckoned, otherwise known as Swedish whitebeam, or service tree. It is rare, virtually impossible, my friend pointed out, for such trees to attain an age of 200 years. So it could not have been this particular one that had been planted at the time of the royal wedding.

All the same, I did not throw the service leaf away.

Les Tilleuls, Villa Jamot, le Vieux Phare (Höedic)

INDEX

CHRONOLOGY

AD 853   First mention of the Cours, a people belonging to the Balt group, who gave their name to Courland.

1198   Founding of the Order of Teutonic Knights at Saint-Jean d'Acre.

1202   Founding of the Order of the Brothers of the Sword.

1237   Merging of the Teutonic Knights with the Brothers of the Sword as the Order of Livonia, the chief protagonist in the *Drang nach Osten* (thrust towards the East), a policy that forced systematic colonization and compulsive evangelization on the local inhabitants.

1245   Conquest of pagan Courland by Dietrich von Grüningen.

1410   Defeat of the Teutonic Knights at the Battle of Tannenberg.

1440   Windau (Ventspils) becomes a member of the Hanseatic League.

1561   Gotthard Kettler, the last Grand Master of the Order of Livonia, becomes Grand Duke of Courland and Semigalia on a hereditary basis, but must pay tribute to the King of Poland. (Courland will be independent only for 234 years.)

1642   Jacob Kettler, Gotthard's grandson, becomes Duke of Courland.

1643   Commercial treaty signed between Courland and France.

1651   Duke Jacob sets up a trading post on the island of St Andrew (today St James) on the River Gambia.

1654   The frigate *Duchess of Courland* sets sail from Windau for the island of Tobago.

1656	Sweden invades Courland, occupies Mitau and takes Duke Jacob prisoner.
1660	Treaty of Oliva; Duke Jacob is freed.
1681	Death of Duke Jacob.
1700	Beginning of the Great Northern Wars between Charles XII and Russia.
1709	Defeat of Charles XII at Pultowa.
1721	Treaty of Nystad between Russia and Sweden. While Poland is being carved up, Russia makes Courland a satellite state and then subjugates it. His Baltic possessions open "a window on Europe" for the tsar.
1726	Maurice de Saxe is elected ruler of Courland.
1737	Death of Ferdinand, last of the Kettler dynasty. Election of Ernst-Johann von Biron, the favourite of Anna Ivanovna, who had become tsarina under the name of Anna I.
1738	Building of the palace of Mitau is begun on the site of a feudal castle.
1740	Death of Tsarina Anna I. Her favourite, Biron, is arrested and sent into exile.
1764	Duke Ernst-Johann returns to Mitau. Casanova is received at court.
1772	Death of Ernst-Johann de Biron. His son Pierre succeeds him and makes Mitau a centre of French culture.
1779	Cagliostro is received at the court of Courland.
1795	Pierre von Biron abdicates. The Duchy of Courland and Semigalia is annexed by Russia.
1799	Louis XVIII arrives at Mitau. Marriage of the Duc d'Angoulême to his cousin Madame Royale.
1801	Louis XVIII is expelled from Courland by Tsar Paul I. Dorothea of Courland, daughter of Pierre, marries Edmond de Talleyrand-Périgord, nephew of the Bishop of Autun.

1804 Louis XVIII's second visit to Mitau.

1807 The Treaty of Tilsit forces Louis XVIII to leave Courland.

1816 Abolition of slavery in Courland.

1855 The writer Eduard von Keyserling is born at Tels Paddern (today Padure).

1904 The Second Pacific Squadron sets sail from Libau to relieve Port Arthur (October).

1905 Red Sunday in St Petersburg. Unrest throughout the Russian empire (January). After a voyage of almost eight months, the Second Pacific Squadron is defeated by the Japanese at Tsushima (May). Peasants' uprising in Courland against the Germano-Baltic barons. Almost 300 mansions and estates are ransacked or destroyed.

1914 Defeat of the Russian army at Tannenberg.

1915 German attack on Courland. Fall of Mitau (August). Policy of Germanization.

1917 Russian Revolution encourages nationalist claims by the Latvians. German attack on the River Daugava (August). Riga captured (September).

1918 Signing of the Treaty of Brest-Litovsk (March). Proclamation of the Republic of Latvia (18 November).

1919 The Bolsheviks seize control of Riga (January). Von der Goltz, who is planning the *Baltikum* (German colonization of the Baltic countries), arrives in Libau (February). The Bolsheviks evacuate Courland. *Coup d'état* against Ulmanis' government (April). French mission under the command of Colonel du Parquet arrives in the harbour of Libau, where the Allied fleet is anchored (20 May). Von der Goltz yields control of Riga. Under the command of Captain Brisson, the Franco-British fleet bombards Riga (October), thus enabling the return of the Ulmanis government. This sounds the death knell for the *Baltikum*.

1920   Signing of the Treaty of Riga between the new Latvian republic and Soviet Russia. Agrarian reforms dispossess the Germano-Baltic nobility of its lands.

1934   *Coup d'état* by Ulmanis.

1939   Signing of the Nazi–Soviet Pact, whose secret clauses anticipate the division of Eastern Europe. Latvia is included within the Soviet sphere (23 August).

1940   The Red Army occupies Riga. The Latvian government is obliged to hand over power to a pro-Soviet government. First deportations of Latvians to Siberia (June).

1941   Following the launch of Operation Barbarossa against the USSR, the Germans are initially greeted as liberators (June).

1943   Founding of the Legion of Volunteers in support of the Germans, numbering as many as 140,000 men.

1944   First Battle of Courland. The Red Army's offensive is halted (October). Battle of Saldus (December).

1945   Large-scale attack by the Red Army to crush the Courland Pocket (March). Last air and sea battle of the Second World War off Liepaja (9 May). Latvia becomes subservient to the USSR.

1948   Massive deportations to Siberia, estimated at 100,000 people.

1989   Fiftieth anniversary of the Nazi–Soviet Pact, which prompted a vast human chain from Tallinn to Vilnius (23 August).

1991   Formal independence of Latvia (21 August).

1999   Vaira Vike-Freiberga (a French speaker) is elected President of the Republic of Latvia (17 June).

2003   Closing of the Ventspils pipeline by the Russians.

2004   Formal entry of Latvia into the European Union. Latvia joins NATO.

2007 Aivars Lembergs, the mayor of Ventspils, accused of abuse of
      power, corruption and money-laundering, is arrested and
      imprisoned (March). He is released a few months later.

2009 Latvia, which showed the healthiest growth in the European
      Union (12.2 per cent in 2006), feels the full force of the
      international economic crisis. Violent demonstrations in
      Riga (January).

NOTES

Page 19: For convenience, the diacritic symbols (accent, cedilla, dash), which are very numerous in Latvian words, are not shown.

Page 28: Published in English in a translation by Grace Frick, in collaboration with the author, by Secker & Warburg (London, 1957). [*Tr.*]

Page 29: The *grand oral* is an important and very demanding public oral examination taken by French students at the end of their university courses, in which candidates are expected to present or defend a given subject in front of a small jury. [*Tr.*]

Page 35: Marguerite Yourcenar, born in Belgium in 1903, was of French aristocratic descent. She is best remembered for her novel *Memoirs of Hadrian* (1951). In 1980, she became the first woman to be elected to the Académie Française. In 1939 she and her partner and translator, Grace Frick, moved to the United States, where they bought a house on Mount Desert Island, off the coast of Maine. Yourcenar died in 1987. [*Tr.*]

Page 40: Jean-Paul Kauffmann's book about his visit to the Kerguelen Islands, translated into English by Patricia Clancy, was published in English as *Voyage to Desolation Island* (London, 2001). [*Tr.*]

Page 42: Literally, "despite ourselves". Still a sensitive subject, the term refers to the 130,000 or more men from Alsace and Lorraine who in August 1942 were forcibly conscripted into the German army. [*Tr.*]

Page 53: The originally German aristocracy, descended from the Teutonic knights, is referred to incorrectly by the generic term "Baltic barons", which creates confusion with the term "Baltic countries", meaning the three nations of Lithuania, Latvia and Estonia (Lithuanian and Latvian are both Baltic languages of Indo-European origin, whereas Estonian is, like Hungarian, Finno-Ugric). It would probably be more correct to use the term "Germano-Baltic barons".

Page 64: Blaise Cendrars (1887–1961), the technically innovative and widely travelled Franco-Swiss poet and writer. (*Tr.*)

Page 66: In June 1941 there were 7,000 Jews living in Liepaja; one year later, there were only 830 (Nadine Fresco, *La Mort des juifs*).

Page 71: The original German title is *Am Südhang*. There does not appear to be a published translation into English. [*Tr.*]

Page 77: *Les Sites de la mémoire russe: Géographie de la mémoire russe*, vol. I (2007).

Page 86: On Sunday, 9 January, 1905, in St Petersburg, troops opened fire on demonstrators led by the popular Orthodox priest Georgij Gapon.

Page 87: "Tsouchima, défaite russe et stupeur occidentale", *Faits et imaginaire de la guerre russo-japonaise, Les Cahiers de l'Exotisme*, no. 5.

Page 96: Only three of Keyserling's novels appear to have been translated into English: *The Curse of the Tarniffs* [*Beate und Mareile*] in 1928, *Tides* [*Wellen*] in 1929, and *Man of God* [*Dumala*] in 1930. [*Tr.*]

Page 110: From the last volume of Ernst Jünger's war diaries, published in France under the title *La Cabane dans la vigne*. It seems that only *Storm and Steel*, his diary of the Great War, has been published in English. [*Tr.*]

Page 117: *Histoire de la vigne et du vin en France* (Paris, 1977).

Page 121: I am most grateful to Anthea Bell for providing me with a translation of the fifth verse of Goethe's poem. [*Tr.*]

Page 127: Gaston Bachelard, *L'Air et les songes* (Paris, 1943).

Page 144: "Cow; rotten; a stab in the back". [*Tr.*]

Page 145: In 1656 Sweden invaded Courland, in order to put pressure on Poland, and seized Mitau, taking Duke Jacob prisoner; he did not return to his duchy until 1660.

Page 153: Mitau (today Jelgava) is in the neighbouring province of Zemgale.

Page 163: *Histoire de l'émigration*, vol. III.

Page 163†: Anne Sommerlat, "Défense, illustration et mise en scène du peuple letton à la fin du XVIIIᵉ siècle", *Cahiers du Mimmoc*, no. 2 (September 2006).

Page 166: Before his return to Paris, Louis XVIII signed a proclamation at Saint-Ouen on 2 May, 1814, which would form the basis for the Constitutional Charter of June 1814. [*Tr.*]

Page 166†: Later Charles X, King of France from 1824 to 1830, following the death of Louis XVIII. Their elder brother was Louis XVI, who was executed during the French Revolution. [*Tr.*]

Page 167: Dominique Fernandez, *La Perle et le croissant* (Paris, 1995).

Page 167†: Philippe Minguet, *L'Ésthétique du rococo* (Paris, 1966), quoted in Victor L. Tapié, *Baroque et classicisme*, 1ˢᵗ edn (Paris, 1957).

Page 170: Readers may be interested to know of Jean-Paul Kauffmann's earlier book, *The Dark Room at Longwood*, translated by Patricia Clancy (London, 1999), which describes his own visit to Saint Helena. [*Tr.*]

Page 170†: Philip Mansel, *Louis XVIII* (London, 1981).

Page 175: Eylau (today Bagrationovsk) was the scene of one of Napoleon's bloodiest battles against the Prussians and the Russians. It took place on 7–8 February, 1807, and was inconclusive. [*Tr.*]

Page 196: From a poem by Peter Suchenwirth, quoted by Sylvain Gougenheim in *Les Chevaliers teutoniques* (Paris, 2007).

Page 196†: Arveds Schwabe, *History of the Latvian People*, Information Bureau of the Latvian Legation in London (Stockholm, 1953).

Page 206: *Wellen* (1911).

Page 212: René Puaux, *Portrait de la Lettonie* (Paris, 1937).

Page 212†: *Souvenirs de Madame Louise-Élisabeth Vigée-Lebrun.*

Page 212‡: "Le Duché de Courlande et l'Aufklärung dans la seconde moitié du XVIIIe siècle: Interactions et representations", PhD thesis, 2005.

Page 213: Marguerite Yourcenar, *Les Yeux ouverts*: *Conversations with Matthieu Galey* (Paris, 1980).

Page 218: See Yves Plasseraud, *Les États baltiques, des societés gigones*, 2nd edn (Paris, 2006).

Page 218†: Award-winning French comic-book creator, writer and film maker, born in Belgrade in 1951. His work has frequently appeared in the American magazine *Heavy Metal*. [*Tr.*]

Page 235: See Roger Stéphane, *Portrait de l'aventurier (Lawrence, Malraux, von Salomon)* (Paris, 2004).

Page 240: Rosalynd Pflaum, *By Influence and Desire: The True Story of Three Extraordinary Women: The Grand Duchess of Courland and her Daughters* New York, 1984).

Page 242: On 15 May, 1796, General Bonaparte made his entry into Milan at the head of the young army that had just marched over the bridge at Lodi, showing the world that, after so many centuries, Caesar and Alexander had a successor. [*Tr.*]

Page 243: The *Cent-Jours* (Hundred Days) refers to the period between 1 March, 1815, when Napoleon returned to France after his exile on Elba, and 22 June, 1815, when his second abdication ushered in the restoration of Louis XVIII. [*Tr.*]

SUGGESTED READING

The majority of the books I have consulted were written in French. I have therefore listed just a small selection of those titles I consider most relevant.

Abols, Guntar *Contribution of History to Latvian Identity* (Nacionalais Apgads, 2002).

Benoist-Méchin, Jacques *Histoire de l'armée allemande*, vol. II: *1919–1938* (Albin Michel, 1938).

Brugis, Dainis *Historisma pilis latvija*, with English summary (Sorosa Fonds-Latvija, 1996).

Jeannin, Pierre *Marchands du nord, espaces et trafics à l'époque modern*, ed. Philippe Braunstein and Jochen Hoock (Presses de l'École Normale Supérieure, 1996).

Manchip White, Jon *Marshals of France: The Life and Times of Maurice, Comte de Saxe, 1696–1750* (Rand McNally, 1962).

Orcier, Pascal *Latvia in Europe*, atlas with foreword by Michel Foucher, bilingual edn (Apgads Zvaigzne ABC, 2005).

Plasseraud, Yves *Les Pays baltes*, foreword by Marc Ferro (Groupement pour les Droits des Minorités, 1990).

Raspe, Rudolph Eric *The Adventures of Baron Münchhausen* (Forgotten Books, 2008).

Rusmanis, S. and Viks, I. *Kurzeme*, bilingual Latvian–English edn (Latvian Encyclopaedia Publishers, 1993).

Thiess, Frank *The Voyage of Forgotten Men (Tsushima)*, trans. Fritz Sallager (Bobbs Merrill, 1937).

Zarans, Albert *Latvijas pilis un muižas: Castles and Manors of Latvia* (n.p., 2006).

ACKNOWLEDGEMENTS

Firstly, I should like to thank Michel Foucher. Apart from the fact that he was kind enough to read my manuscript, he provided me with many leads. His analyses of Courland and Latvia, always relevant, were of particular value. I am grateful to him, too, for having recommended to me "the house on the lake", which I count among my very best memories of Courland. I am also grateful to Yves Plasseraud, Rolands Lappuke and Astra Skrabane.

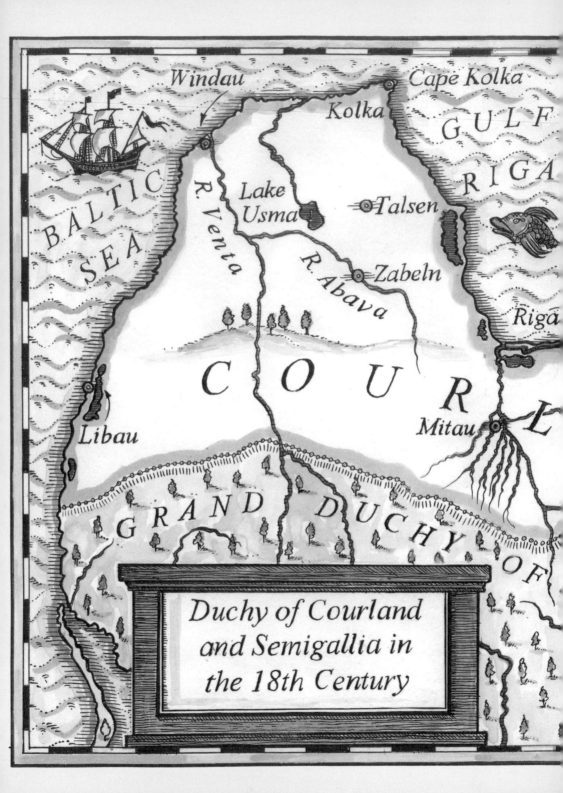

Duchy of Courland
and Semigallia in
the 18th Century